Intergenerational Programs: Imperatives, Strategies, Impacts, Trends

D0209657

Intergenerational Programs: Imperatives, Strategies, Impacts, Trends

Sally Newman, PhD
Steven W. Brummel, MA
Editors

The Haworth Press
New York • London

Intergenerational Programs: Imperatives, Strategies, Impacts, Trends has also been published as *Journal of Children in Contemporary Society*, Volume 20, Numbers 3/4 1989.

The Haworth Press, Inc., 10 Alice Street, Binghamton, NY 13904-1580
EUROSPAN/Haworth, 3 Henrietta Street, London WC2E 8LU England

Library of Congress Cataloging-in-Publication Data

Intergenerational programs : imperatives, strategies, impacts, trends / Sally Newman, Steven W. Brummel, editors.
    p. cm.
    "Has also been published as Journal of Children in Contemporary Society, Volume 20, Number 3/4 1989.
    Includes bibliographies and index.
    ISBN 0-86656-773-9
    1. Age groups — United States. 2. Integenerational relations — United States. 3. United States — Social policy. 4. Social work with children — United States. 5. Social work with the aged — United States. I. Newman, Sally. II. Brummel, Steven W.
HM131.I543 1989
305.2 — dc19

89-1775
CIP

Intergenerational Programs: Imperatives, Strategies, Impacts, Trends

CONTENTS

ABOUT THE EDITORS

Steven Brummel and Sally Newman are both renowned pioneers in the development, implementation, and expansion of intergenerational program models. They hold leadership positions in national and international organizations dealing with aging and intergenerational issues, have published widely, and enjoy international reputations for their work.

Sally Newman, PhD, is Founder and Executive Director of Generations Together, a program of the University of Pittsburgh's Center for Social and Urban Research, where she is responsible for developing intergenerational programs and disseminating information, both locally and nationally, on their development and research efforts. Dr. Newman holds a joint faculty position as Senior Research Associate at the Center and as Clinical Instructor in Psychiatry at the University of Pittsburgh's Western Psychiatric Institute and Clinic. She has conducted some of the seminal research in the field and has published papers on various aspects of intergenerational program development and evaluation. Dr. Newman has lectured in universities in the United States and abroad, and she has conducted workshops and presented papers at national conferences sponsored by child care, aging, and education organizations.

Steven W. Brummel, MA, is President and Chairman of the Board of Directors of the Elvirita Lewis Foundation, where he presides over the foundation's efforts of intergenerational programming, elder productivity, and cross-cultural programs. He administers the foundation's operation of three intergenerational child care centers and a Job Training and Partnership Act Older worker Program. Mr. Brummel is a convening board member of the International Council on Aging. He was a speaker at the 1981 White House Conference on Aging and at the 1982 United Nations World Assembly on Aging. In 1974, he was appointed by California Governor George Deukmejian to the Governor's Task Force on Long-Term Care. Mr. Brummel currently serves on the Organizing Committee Advisory Group for the XIV International Congress of Gerontology to be held in Acapulco, Mexico in June 1989.

Foreword

We are living today in a divided, changing society, frequented by contending special interests and conflicting goals. Laws and public policies directed to the public interest are at best compromised by these special interests.

A changing demography has accelerated possible conflict and competition between the old and the young. More people are living longer than ever before in retirement homes and communities where no children are allowed. The Older American Act established to provide benefits and services for the elderly has codified age segregation.

Aging is a universal human experience shared by all living creatures. All are born of seed, mature, bear progeny, wither and die. The experience should unite us but in the western developed world old age is considered a pathological state and people have become segregated by age, as well as by social class, income and ethnicity. Age segregation has separated the old from the young and violated the continuity and wholeness of the life cycle.

The editors and authors of this timely intergenerational volume describe the creative ways in which age segregation can be eradicated. They point out the benefits for all when the old and the young come together. Generations Together, the Gray Panthers and other intergenerational groups on university campuses and in communities are demonstrating the broad personal social benefits of generational cooperation. The generations are teaching and learning together on college campuses, discovering the values of continuing education. Old people are sharing their experiences in public schools where they are mentors and role models for many young people who grow up apart from grandparents. Young children and teenagers are working on oral history projects in retirement homes. Old and young learn and live together on intergenerational retreats.

The strategies and policies the editors and authors record are changing personal lives, families and human service delivery systems as well as social policy. They have recognized how much the young and the old need each other and how essential sharing is to survival. New social theory and policies are being forged to accomplish this goal.

The historical perspective and experience of old people and the energy and idealism of young people must be linked to deal with the monumental societal problems that endanger our world. We live on the brink of destruction of ourselves and the planet. We are spending a million dollars a minute on nuclear weapons; we are poisoning the oceans and the air; we are scarring the land in search of energy and profitable cash crops. The old and the young are most free to initiate change and take the risks to be advocates of peace and justice. We have nothing to lose!

Margaret E. Kuhn
Founder and National Convenor
GRAY PANTHERS

Preface

This volume was conceived as a theoretical and practical argument for focusing national attention on the need for expanding opportunities for intergenerational exchange. The editors believe that the myriad benefits of intergenerational interactions can strengthen the fabric of our societal structure if a comprehensive national strategy for intergenerational programming and exchange is developed.

In the past few years, we have seen the emergence of published articles and books with intergenerational themes and annotated bibliographies reporting on the array of literature featuring intergenerational issues and compendiums of exemplary intergenerational programs. By bringing together the various elements that are integral to the understanding of intergenerational programming and exchange, *Intergenerational Programs: Imperatives, Strategies, Impacts, Trends* raises to another level of consciousness issues related to intergenerational programs. It presents a view of this emerging field of study from the historical, developmental, socio-political, program development, evaluation and research perspectives.

The editors intend that the presentation of these intergenerational perspectives be useful to professionals and advocates who work with children and the aged as well as to the systems and agencies that represent these two generations. We suggest, also, that confluence or mutuality of interests exists between those concerned with the needs and capacities of children and older adults, and this mutuality is the rationale for intergenerational programming advocacy in the decades ahead.

Intergenerational programs create the potential for a variety of successful interventions using the talents and expertise of professionals working at both ends of the life cycle. The editors postulate, furthermore, that a healthy, mutually beneficial interaction occurs between young and old participants in intergenerational programs.

This monograph will bring together in a cohesive and orderly fashion, the thinking and experience of those who have studied and worked with intergenerational programming over the last three decades. The monograph will address several seminal issues inherent in the growth of this new area of investigation. Of concern are the underlying issues of: competition for federal dollars between old and young; the history of interaction between young and old in western culture; cross-cultural issues; the status of research; and finally the human development life cycle and its effect on intergenerational programming and public policy considerations.

The discussion of these issues and related topics comprise the format of this volume which is divided into four parts. Part I addresses the imperatives for focusing attention on intergenerational programming and exchange from historical, developmental, cross-cultural, societal and public policy perspectives. Part II focuses on program implementation and evaluation, education and training, the role of systems in intergenerational programs and exemplary programs. Part III examines the impact of intergenerational programs on both the old and the young and presents issues related to current and future research. Finally, Part IV considers the federal role in intergenerational issues in the context of national health care, and presents an intergenerational perspective in relationship to its importance to both today's and tomorrow's children and families.

The editors hope that this book will offer a rationale for public support on behalf of intergenerational programming and exchange and will encourage continued efforts in program development and research in this field. As H. R. Moody and R. Disch stated so eloquently (see this edition),

> Both young and old are to be understood as members of an enduring historical community, a public world, existing before their birth and remaining after their departure from the scene. Each stage of the life course — youth, adulthood, old age — has its proper task in transmitting or assimilating the lessons of the past in order to create a better future: in short, to recreate the foundations of the common good.

We would like to thank all the authors who contributed manuscripts for the volume and give special thanks to the staff of Generations Together and the Elvirita Lewis Foundation for their efforts in making this edition a reality.

To the staff from Generations Together: Laurie Eck who facilitated the correspondence and contacts with the guest authors; to Edith Allen, Kathleen Bocian, Barbara Howe and Janet Wilson for their assistance in writing, editing and reviewing; and to Charlotte Siuda, Lily Recchio, Florence Hanley and Virginia Wilmes for their untiring secretarial assistance. To the staff of the Elvirita Lewis Foundation: Shari ReVille, Sallie Johnson and Robin Lewellyn for assistance in writing and editing and to Lynn Dawson and Handel Caballero for secretarial assistance. Special thanks to the editor of *Journal of Children in Contemporary Society*, Mary Frank, for her enthusiasm, support and counselling.

Steven W. Brummel, MA
Editor

A History of Intergenerational Programs

Sally Newman, PhD

Since the mid 1960s, gerontologists, psychologists, educators and specialists in human development have been reporting an increase in the number of elderly persons in our population, a growth in the number of age segregated communities, and a decrease in consistent and frequent interactions among younger and older members of our families. The outcomes of these related social phenomena have effected the lives of our elderly and our children.

For our elderly, there has been (an observed) decline in self-esteem, and self-worth, and an increase in feelings of loneliness. For our children and youth, there has been an observed loss of the traditional elder/child nurturing, a loss of cultural and historical connections, and an increase in their fear of aging. Age segregation, furthermore, seems to have resulted in an increase in myths and stereotypes between the young and the old. These trends have promoted the development of a new social service field "Intergenerational Programming and Exchange." The evolution of this field is represented by a series of actions involving the collaboration of local, state and national agencies, public and private sector systems and community groups.

This paper will present a chronology of significant events and initiatives that contributed to the growth of intergenerational programs and exchange, a field whose time has come and whose impact is evident in communities throughout the country.

Sally Newman is Clinical Instructor of Psychiatry at the Western Psychiatric Institute, University of Pennsylvania, Senior Research Associate at the University Center for Social and Urban Research, and Executive Director of Generations Together, 811 William Pitt Union, University of Pittsburgh, Pittsburgh, PA 15260.

CHRONOLOGY

1963: Foster Grandparents Program (FGP). The concept of intergenerational programming was introduced with the establishment of the FGP by the Office of Economic Opportunity as a Community Action Project. The initial intent of the program was to demonstrate the capabilities of lower income older persons. However, in 1965, when the FGP program became a member of the volunteer ACTION network, its focus was described as an intergenerational model concerned with matching of lower income, healthy older adults to children with special or exceptional needs.

1963: Adopt a Grandparent Program. The grandparent of grandparenting programs was developed at the P. K. Yonge Laboratory School, University of Florida (Whitley, 1976). It involved weekly class visits by young children to a neighboring convalescent home. An adaptation of this model has been integrated into the programming of the Beverly Nursing Home Network and is being implemented throughout their system.

1967-69: Serve and Enrich Retirement by Volunteer Experience (SERVE). This program was established on Staten Island, New York as a project of the Community Service Society enabling persons over sixty to provide volunteer service to the community. Funded initially with grants from the federal government, local foundations and the Community Service Society, SERVE grew from a project with twenty-three older volunteers working with children and young adults at a residential home for the mentally retarded to a project involving 1,500 senior volunteers working in ninety agencies of which the majority serve children and their families. The success of SERVE was the catalyst for the establishment of the Retired Senior Volunteer Program (RSVP). In 1985, SERVE merged with RSVP in New York City and became part of a five borough program.

1969: Retired Senior Volunteer Program (RSVP). The RSVP was created as a national program authorized under Title 4, Part A, of the reauthorization act of the Older Americans Act of 1965. The SERVE program (note previous citation), which was the catalyst for this legislation, became a prototype for many of the RSVP agencies throughout the country (Sainer, 1971). Today there are 750 RSVP programs with 400,000 senior volunteers.

1969: National Center for Service-Learning. This center was established as the National Student Volunteer Program and acts as an advocate for the development and expansion of student volunteers and service-learning programs with a focus on service to the elderly. It offered free training programs, resource materials, and technical assistance for high school and college community service program coordinators (National, 1980). Students from fifty universities in disciplines such as nursing, social work, vocational education, rehabilitation counselling, etc., provided weekly service to the elderly in their community. Though significantly curtailed in size since 1982, the program, now called Student Community Service, continues to provide opportunities for interaction between college youth and older persons in approximately thirty communities.

1970: The Gray Panthers. Maggie Kuhn convened the Gray Panthers as an advocacy group involving active collaboration between younger and older members of our society in order to address social policy issues. Ageism in society is one of the basic issues addressed by the Gray Panthers.

1975: U. S. Office of Education and U.S. Administration on Aging. An agreement was signed between these two federal agencies that established guidelines for using the nation's schools to provide a variety of educational, recreational, nutritional and volunteer opportunities for the nation's elderly. An outgrowth of this federal initiative was a series of memoranda signed between the Secretaries of Aging and Education in 14 states. These memoranda fostered regional meetings between members of aging and education networks to develop strategies for providing service to older Americans through their involvement in schools.

1975: Louis Harris and Associates. Data reported from a survey "Myths and Reality of Aging in America" conducted for the National Council on the Aging, estimated that more than 40,000

Americans over 65 years of age were serving as volunteers in public education systems throughout the United States.

1976: California Department of Education. With a grant from the Department of Education, the first aging education program was developed and introduced into the curriculum for children in grades K-12 in the California Public Schools. This demonstration project which included older persons as resources in the classroom was implemented in 43 classrooms throughout the state (Marshall, 1985).

1976: Teaching-Learning Communities. This intergenerational program was developed as a model to bring elders, their crafts and their caring into the public schools of Ann Arbor, Michigan. The model has been adapted and replicated in a variety of communities across the United States (Tice, 1986).

1977-79: State of Florida. Legislation was passed to support the creation of a school volunteer network throughout the state. The network included the community's senior citizens who became an essential part of the classroom instructional teaching team in all early childhood classrooms (Florida, 1979). Currently over 15,000 senior citizens are involved in K-3 classrooms throughout the state of Florida.

1978: The Edna McConnell Clark Foundation. An award of $10,000,000 was made to six major school systems (Boston, Los Angeles, Miami, New York, Seattle, St. Louis) with the charge to develop, over a three year period, intergenerational programs that would involve older persons as volunteers who would contribute directly to support the growth and learning of youth in school settings. This grant resulted in the emergence of the largest and most significant intergenerational program network in the United States (older persons as volunteers in public education). A 1982 survey conducted for the National School Volunteer Program reported that several thousand urban, suburban and rural school systems throughout the country regularly involved over 1,000,000 older residents in a variety of direct volunteer roles within the public school network.

1978: Messiah Village, Mechanicsburg, Pennsylvania. A model multi-care retirement center that included an intergenerational component was established in Mechanicsburg, Pennsylvania. Housed within Messiah Village was to be a child care center whose daily schedule included interaction between the children and the older residents. This unique intergenerational project has become the prototype for other long-term care or retirement centers.

1978: Generations Together, University of Pittsburgh. This was the first university program that was developed to focus its work exclusively on the concept of intergenerational exchange. The goals of this program were to develop intergenerational program models, to research their outcomes, and to disseminate information on program development and research. The program has developed a variety of models that are being implemented in Pennsylvania and other states and has conducted and reported on evaluations and research of selected models.

1979: Intergenerational Child Care Centers. The California Intergenerational Child Care Act of 1979 voted into law support for the development of two intergenerational child care centers that would be modeled after a 1976 intergenerational child care center model jointly funded by the state and the Elvirita Lewis Foundation. These three successful intergenerational child care models prompted the preparation of the California Intergenerational Child Care Act of 1985 that passed the legislature unanimously but was vetoed by the governor.

1980: Close Harmony. This was the first intergenerational film produced and widely distributed. It presented the evolution of a unique program model. "Close Harmony" effectively described the development of procedures involved in creating an intergenerational choir whose participants, members of a senior center and students at a private school, developed important and meaningful relationships.

1980: National Council on the Aging (NCoA). A national effort to foster an intergenerational program network was initiated by NCoA. It convened a series of mini-conferences throughout the

United States whose purpose was to develop strategies for linking the generations. The outcome of this effort was the preparation of a position paper "Strategies for Linking the Generations" that was prepared for the 1981 White House Conference on Aging (Strategies, 1981).

1981: The White House Conference on Aging. Conferees of the WHCoA prepared and submitted to Congress two position papers related to intergenerational interaction: (a) "Challenging Age Stereotypes in the Media," a document that reported on a WHCoA Mini-Conference in which media experts and anti-ageist advocates worked together to develop a strategy for improving the representation of older persons in all aspects of the media (White House Conference on Aging, 1981), and (b) "Older Americans as a National Growing Resource," a report from the WHCoA Technical Committee that described existing opportunities for older persons as active participants in society and recommended strategies for the government, the private sector, and the volunteer sector for maintaining this national resource (White House Conference on Aging, 1981).

1981: Intergenerational Clearinghouse Newsletter. RSVP (Dane County, Wisconsin) was funded by ACTION to establish a national clearinghouse newsletter on intergenerational programs and issues. The newsletter gathered information on RSVP, Foster Grandparents, VISTA, and other programs that linked the generations. The newsletter, which currently receives local funding, reports two times annually and has become a forum for the exchange of information among the intergenerational program network. It also promulgated the bringing together of isolated local intergenerational programs into this network (Staff, 1987).

1982: State Departments of Aging and Education. A memoranda of understanding was signed between the Departments of Aging and Education in California, Florida, and Pennsylvania. These memoranda addressed the need to provide educational experiences that promoted the understanding of the aging process and that provided opportunities for exchange between the generations.

1982: The World Assembly on Aging in Vienna. The final report of this international meeting expressed a deep concern regarding the alienation and generational discontinuity in societies accepting western models of industrialization, bureaucratization, occupational and organizational complexities. ". . . they recommend the encouraging of activities and programs to enhance generational solidarity" (Oriol, 1982).

1982: Office of Human Development Services (OHDS). A request for proposals was announced through the OHDS Coordinated Discretionary Funds Program. Funds for this program were provided by the Administration on Aging, Administration for Children, Youth and Families, Administration on the Developmental Disabilities, Administration for Native Americans and the Office of Human Development Services. The proposals focused on intergenerational solutions to some of the issues concerning the constituencies served by the aforementioned administrations. Similar RFPs have appeared annually since 1982.

1984: AARP Parent Aide Program. AARP received an OHDS coordinated discretionary grant award to develop a demonstration intergenerational program "Older Volunteers in Partnership with Parents to Prevent Child Abuse and Neglect." This demonstration was implemented in five child abuse projects and involved 40 volunteers working with 135 children in 63 families.

1985: The 99th Congress. A companion bill "Intergenerational Education Volunteer Network Act of 1985" was introduced into the 99th Congress by Congressman Ed Roybal (House Bill 1587) and by Senator Carl Levin (Senate Bill 1022). The bill which was cosponsored by Republicans and Democrats in both houses established a senior citizen volunteers tutorial network in public school systems. It provided opportunities for senior citizens to work in elementary and secondary schools and in homes with educationally disadvantaged children and their families. The bill was referred to committee and remained there during the term of the 99th Congress with no further action. It is being considered for reintroduction in the 100th session of Congress.

1984-1986: Intergenerational Program Surveys. Several surveys were published that reported on the current status of intergenerational programs in the United States. These surveys presented profiles of representative programs at the state and the national levels and were made available to local, state and national organizations (Murphy, 1984; Pennsylvania, 1984; Ventura-Merkel, 1984; California, 1984).

1984-87: Statewide Networks. Intergenerational statewide and regional networks were created in California, Illinois, Massachusetts, New Jersey, New York, Pennsylvania, and Wisconsin. The structure and direction of these networks were based upon their membership and the source of the leadership in each state. The networks included collaboration between local agencies and systems representing aging, education and child care (e.g., RSVP, local school districts and NAEYC), State Departments of Aging, Education, and Public Welfare, and consortiums of local intergenerational programs.

California — 1984-86. With funding from Luke B. Hancock and other foundations and corporations, several workshops were convened to support the work of intergenerational programs in Northern California and to establish a Northern California Intergenerational Program Network (Staff, 1985). This network is being maintained through scheduled meetings and a newsletter.

Illinois — October 1987. The Illinois Department of Aging held a series of seminars in the spring of 1987 with eleven universities and the voluntary sector. The seminars were designed to address the issue of Generational Equity and the New Generation Gap. The seminars titled "Interdependence of the Generations" presented recommendations to the state on how to mobilize support for a productive state policy that would unite the generations and move toward family policies across the age spectrum (Illinois, 1987).

Massachusetts — May 1987. Following several months of planning by a convening group representing numerous organizations, the Massachusetts Intergenerational Network (MIN) was formally established as a membership organization. MIN was a statewide coalition of people of all ages who believed that interaction and cooperation among generations contribute to the good of individuals and the well being of society (Staff, 1987).

New Jersey — 1985. The Division on Aging in the Department of Community Affairs promoted the concept of intergenerational programs to statewide education and social service agencies and to community based organizations. As an intergenerational program advocate the department has convened workshops on program development and is a resource for both written and media materials. It has supported the development of intergenerational programs by funding three demonstration projects which have been sustained through subsequent private or public funds.

New York — 1986. A policy statement was adopted by the New York State Board of Regents that challenged educators to develop a comprehensive strategy to mobilize the capacity of the educational system in addressing the multiple needs of the aging population in the context of existing social and economic conditions. Major policy recommendations advanced by the state were: to foster administrative and community intergenerational cooperation and exchange, to enhance the coordination of services for the elderly by strengthening the links between education, aging and other state level agencies, to involve the elderly as active participants in the society, and to educate students at all levels about aging (Educational, 1986).

Pennsylvania — 1982-1988. The Pennsylvania Department of Aging promoted the development and networking of intergenerational programs through several initiatives;

- funding annually the development of intergenerational demonstration models each of which prepared a manual to be used for dissemination and networking activities
- preparing a department recommendation for all Area Agencies on Aging (AAAs) which encouraged their involvement in the development of intergenerational programs (1982)
- signing a Memoranda of Understanding with the Pennsylvania Department of Public Welfare and the Pennsylvania Association of Non-Profit Homes for the Aged encouraging collaboration in the development of intergenerational programs (1982)

—preparing a resource guide describing 73 existing examples of intergenerational programs in the commonwealth. The guide is designed to promote networking throughout the commonwealth (1984)

1984—Child Care and Aging Network Program. Generations Together received an OHDS coordinated discretionary grant award to facilitate the development of intergenerational child care programs linking the child care and aging network in the commonwealth of Pennsylvania. The project was designed to foster, at a statewide level, the systematic linking of two systems in a collaborative intergenerational program effort. Through this effort, over sixty intergenerational child care models emerged that involve collaboration among a variety of child care and aging network agencies (e.g., child care centers, head start programs, senior centers, and nursing homes). An informal network was created among these models in several regions of the Commonwealth (Staff, 1986).

1985—The Governor issued a statement on Public Policy Guidelines that encouraged the Departments of Aging, Public Welfare and Education to work together to increase the availability of child care services through models involving senior citizens.

1986—With funding from the Philadelphia Foundation, the Center for Intergenerational Learning (a program of Temple University's Institute on Aging) created the Delaware Valley Intergenerational Network (DELVIN) (Staff, 1986). DELVIN brought together networks of agencies serving the youth, the elderly, and religious and volunteer sectors to prioritize their needs and identify gaps in their service delivery.

1988—The Governor initiates a plan for establishing on-site day care centers for children of state employees and encourages the use of intergenerational program models in these sites.

Wisconsin — 1981-87.

1981 — A meeting between community education, public education, and the Department of Aging was held to initiate a discussion on intergenerational efforts in the State.

1983 — A booklet was published "Intergenerational Programming in Wisconsin Schools" that described a variety of programs in the Wisconsin schools.

1984 — Workshops were held throughout the state involving the aging and public school networks.

1985 — A consortium of Wisconsin agencies assumed the leadership in the Wingspread Intergenerational Conference held in Racine, Wisconsin. This conference involved the participation of intergenerational programs throughout the country and produced a "How To" guide book to assist local organizations in the development of intergenerational programs (Thorpe, 1985).

1986 — A statewide Intergenerational Network Conference is convened involving schools, aging and community groups.

1987 — A statewide survey is conducted to determine the kind of intergenerational activities and programs available in the state.

1985-87: Intergenerational Program Guide Manuals. Several guides were published to support the development of intergenerational programs and were made available to the intergenerational program networks throughout the country. These guides describe procedures for implementing a variety of intergenerational program models (e.g., preschoolers and elders in long-term care settings, preschoolers and elders in child care settings, school age children and elders in public schools, and youth with the frail elderly in nursing home settings) (Barrett, 1986; Cohen, 1981; Beverly, 1984; Johnson, 1980; Hegeman, 1985; Kramer, 1986; Newman, 1987; Lyons, 1985; Reed, 1982; Spitler [nd]; Ventura-Merkle, 1983).

1986: Administration on Aging/National Public-Private Intergenerational Initiative. A contract was signed between the Administration on Aging (AoA) and the Elvirita Lewis Foundation (ELF) to support the development of a variety of intergenerational projects in nine communities from Massachusetts to California. Each project was selected and funded by a local foundation with matching funds from the AoA contract. The project administration was assigned to ELF who functioned as the initiative secretariat and with the assistance of the consortium of collaborating foundations, coordinates the reporting of the project to the AoA.

1986: Generations United. A consortium of national agencies joined together to advocate for public policies and programs that recognize the interdependence of children, youth, families and the elderly. One hundred organizations were members of Generations United supporting and participating in a variety of advocacy activities (Liederman, 1987).

1987: United States Congress Child Care Legislation. Three Senate bills, #1885 — Act for Better Child Care (ABC) — introduced by Senator Christopher Dodd, #2084 and #2085 — Child Care Services Improvement Act — introduced by Senator Orin Hatch, identified the need to include older persons as child care providers in the plan to improve the quality and quantity of child care service in the United States. These bills were introduced during the late winter 1987 and were referred to committee early in 1988. It is hoped that by publication time of this edition, a comprehensive child care act will have passed both houses of Congress.

1987: Pennsylvania State Assembly. Intergenerational legislation was introduced into the Pennsylvania Assembly which was co-sponsored by Representatives Ron Cowell and Jon Fox and supported by members of both parties. "Intergenerational Teaching Programs," an amendment to Public School Code Bill 1949, was designed to provide funds to educational systems (primary, secondary and higher education) for innovative teaching strategies that would result in intergenerational programs in schools. The bill was introduced November 1987 and referred to committee for review. It is hoped that by the publication time of this edition, the Intergenerational Education bill will have been voted into law in Pennsylvania.

1984-88: Expansion of Intergenerational Models. In response to the growing needs of our urban populations of children, young families and elderly, a variety of new intergenerational programs have been developed to address some of the problems in our cities. Programs focusing on at-risk children and their families, teenage pregnancy, multicultural and homeless families, abused and abandoned children, self-care children, children with special needs, elders in adult day care and elders in the work force, are among the newer intergenerational programs being developed in the 1980s. In addition to these new models, local efforts in schools, child care centers and nursing homes continue to be developed in urban, suburban and rural communities.

Though this chronology focused on some of the intergenerational program efforts which have had an impact on public policy, which are prototypes for future programs, or which demonstrated their ability for replication, we would like to acknowledge the hundreds of local intergenerational programs whose existence has sustained the momentum of intergenerational program efforts by illustrating their ability to improve the quality of life for all the generations in their communities. We hope that the information provided in this chronology can become a catalyst that motivates local programs to increase their visibility and to participate in a public policy effort to provide statewide or national support of intergenerational program efforts.

CONCLUSION

This chronology of events and initiatives in the field of intergenerational programs and exchange portrays a consistent growth in interest in this field from diverse local and national constituencies. This growth seems to reinforce the need to maintain connections between the generations that Margaret Mead said were "essential for the mental health and stability of a nation." The varied initiatives and their varied origins suggest that we are involved in a broad based effort that has the potential for fostering some major changes in society which can contribute to the stability of our nation.

REFERENCES

Barrett, D., Myers, R., Kramer, C., Newman, S., & Mullins, J. (1986). *Intergenerational volunteer program in special education: A manual for implementation*. Pittsburgh, PA: University of Pittsburgh. Generations Together.

The Beverly Foundation. *A time and place for sharing: A practical guide for developing intergenerational programs*. (1984). South Pasadena, CA: Author.

California. State Department of Education. (1984). *Young and old together: A resource directory of intergenerational programs*. (1984). Sacramento: Author.

Cohen, M., Hardgrove, C., & Rosen, K. (1981). *The intergenerational care giving program: A replication manual*. San Francisco, CA: University of California, School of Nursing, Department of Family Health Care Nursing.

Educational elements of a comprehensive state policy on aging. (1986, December). Albany, NY: The University of the State of New York.

Florida. Department of Education. (1979). *Interlock, Florida school volunteer program directory, 1979-1980*. Tallahassee: Author.

Hegeman, C. (1985). *Child care in long-term care settings*. Albany, NY: Foundation for Long Term Care.

Illinois Department of Aging. (1987, October). *Uniting the generations . . . Moving states toward family policies across the age spectrum*. Springfield: Author.

Johnson, S. & Siegel, W. *Bridging generations: A handbook for intergenerational child care* (1980). Palm Springs: The Elvirita Lewis Foundation, Elder Press.

Kramer, C. & Newman, S. (1986). *Senior citizen school volunteer program: Manual for implementation*. Albany, NY: Center for the Study of Aging.

Liederman, D. & Ossofsky, J. (1987, April). *An open letter to members of Generations United*. Newsline, *1* (1), 1. (A newsletter published by Generations United, % Child Welfare League of America, 440 First St., NW, Suite 310, Washington DC 20001-2085.)

Lyons, C. & Newman, S. (1983). *How to develop an intergenerational service-learning program at a nursing home*. Pittsburgh, PA: University of Pittsburgh, Generations Together.

Marshall, M. (1985). *Development of intergenerational education in California*. 8210 Varna Avenue, Van Nuys, CA 91402: Author.

Murphy, M. (1984). *A guide to intergenerational programs*. Washington, DC: National Association of State Units on Aging.

National Center for Service-Learning. (1980). *Planning by objections: A manual for student community service program coordinators*. ACTION. Pamphlet #4000, 15, 10/80. Washington, DC: U. S. Government Printing Office.

Newman, S., Kramer, C., Lyons, C., O'Kane, R., Siegel, E., & Robinson, V. (1987). *Manual for developing intergenerational programs in schools*. Alexandria, VA: National School Volunteer Program.

Oriol, W. (1982). Aging in all nations. *A Special Report on the United Nations*

World Assembly on Aging: Vienna, Austria. July 26-August 6. Washington, DC: National Council on the Aging.

Pennsylvania. Department of Aging. (1984). *Reaching across the years: Selected intergenerational programs in Pennsylvania*. Harrisburg, PA: Author.

Reed, R. & Spieker, D. (1982). *Growing (older) together: Project independence, community resource guide*. Minneapolis, MN: American Red Cross, Minneapolis Area Chapter.

Sainer, J. & Zander, M. (1971). *SERVE: Older volunteers in community service*. New York: Community Service Society of New York.

Spitler, B.J. & Kobata, F. (nd). *Project Y.E.S.: A replication manual for high school use serving the frail elderly*. Los Angeles: University of Southern California, Andrus Gerontology Center, Institute for Policy and Program Development.

Staff. (1986, Spring). Delaware Valley intergenerational network. *Interchange, A newsletter*. (a newsletter published by: Center for Intergenerational Learning, Institute on Aging, Temple University, 1601 N. Broad St., Philadelphia, PA 19122).

Staff. (1987, November). Intergenerational programming development in Wisconsin. *Intergenerational Clearinghouse, 5* (2), 2-3. (a newsletter published by: Intergenerational Clearinghouse Newsletter, RSVP of Dane County, Inc., 540 W. Olin Ave., Madison, WI 53715).

Staff. (1986, Spring). Introducing Joining Together. *Joining Together 1*, (1) (a newsletter published by: Generations Together, University of Pittsburgh, 811 Wm. Pitt Union, Pittsburgh, PA 15260).

Staff. (1987, Spring/Summer). Massachusetts network formed. *Linkages, 2* (2), 1. (a newsletter published by: Center for Understanding Aging, Framingham State College, Framingham, MA 01701).

Staff. (1985, Spring). Update on the intergenerational program network. (a newsletter published by: Project Joy, 6421 Telegraph Ave., Oakland, CA 94609) *Project Joy: Joining older and younger, Newsletter*.

Strategies for linking the generations. (1981). Washington, DC: National Council on the Aging.

Thorp, K. (1985). *Intergenerational programs: A resource for community renewal*. Madison: Wisconsin Positive Youth Development Initiative.

Tice, C. & Warren, B. (1986). *T-LC coordinators handbook teaching-learning communities*. Ypsilanti, MI: Eastern Michigan University, Institute for the Study of Children and Families.

Ventura-Merkel, K. & Parks, E. (1984). *Intergenerational programs: A catalog of profiles*. Washington, DC: National Council on the Aging.

Ventura-Merkel, K. & Lidoff, L. (1983). *Program innovation in aging: Volume VIII, Community planning for intergenerational programming*. Washington, DC: National Council on the Aging.

White House Conference on Aging. (1981). *Older Americans as a growing national resource*. Washington, DC: U. S. Government Printing Office. (GPO 720-019/6886)

White House Conference on Aging. (1981). *Challenging are stereotypes in the media*. Washington, DC. U. S. Government Printing Office. (GPO 720-019/6927)

Whitley, E., Duncan, R., McKenzie, P., & Sledjecki, S. (1976). *From time to time: A record of young children's relationships with the aged*. Gainesville: P.K. Yonge Laboratory School, College of Education, University of Florida.

PART I:
IMPERATIVES

Introduction

By the 21st century, the Western world anticipates a population in which approximately 16% of the people are over 60 years of age. Typical living patterns of this population, most of whom will not be employed, will result in interaction with persons of the same age cohort. In the 21st century, we may also expect an increase in single parent and working parent families whose living patterns stereotypically result in interaction with other younger families. An anticipated outcome for both older and younger persons will be generational isolation. Similar anticipated trends in the underdeveloped countries will result in several universal concerns that emerge because of the lack of exchange between the generations.

Part I of this volume addresses some of the imperatives that suggest the need for intergenerational programs.

In the *Historical Imperative*, Peter Stearns provides an overview of the "Historical Trends in Intergenerational Contacts" over the last 400 years of Western civilization and suggests the historical appropriateness for intergenerational programs at this time. In the *Developmental Imperative*, Marsha Crites examines "Child Development and Intergenerational Programming," by presenting a review of Erik Erikson's developmental stages of children and youth in relationship to children's need for intergenerational contact. Shari M. ReVille in "Young Adulthood to Old Age: Looking at Intergenerational Possibilities from a Human Development Perspective," expands this discussion of the relationship between developmental needs and intergenerational programs by focusing on the later developmental stages in the Erikson human development paradigm.

The *Cross-Cultural Imperative* is examined by Marta Sotomayor in "The Hispanic Elderly and the Intergenerational Family," which outlines the current demographic and economic pressures on older Hispanics and the effect of those pressures on the traditional Hispanic extended family. Ken Tout in "Intergenerational Exchange in

Developing Countries" discusses the issues that are emerging in developing countries in which the phenomenon of the greying of the population is occurring during a 20 year period in contrast to a 200 year period in which the same phenomenon evolved in the developed nations. He describes the impact of this rapid change on generational roles and postulates that this trend is creating an imperative for intergenerational cooperative efforts to replace historical family supports.

The *Societal Imperative* is examined by David Nee in "The Intergenerational Movement: A Social Imperative" which looks at today's social isolation, intergenerational conflict and the future labor shortages. Together, these factors become the catalysts for intergenerational cooperation. Eric R. Kingson in "The Social Policy Implications of Intergenerational Programming and Exchange" focuses on the growing need for intergenerational approaches to public policy.

The last section of Part I, The *Public Policy Imperative* includes "Intergenerational Programming in Public Policy" by Harry R. Moody and Robert Disch which offers a rationale for public support for intergenerational programming. They postulate that the growing need for a public "ideal of citizenship" provides a structure and rationale for personal and group responsibility for generational interactions. Paul S. Nathanson in "A Political Imperative for Intergenerational Programs" suggests that both advocates for the elderly and for children should participate in forming the future intergenerational agenda.

Sally Newman, PhD
Steven W. Brummel, MA

Historical Trends
in Intergenerational Contacts

Peter N. Stearns, PhD

SUMMARY. This paper presents a sobering historical perspective in which the author presents a picture of the pre-industrial and industrial periods in Western societies in which a positive intergenerational model was not in evidence. Contemporary events, however, in an advanced society such as the United States may provide the basis for a balance between the young and old in which each can find from each other needed strengths and important functions.

In a rapidly-aging society, where signs of tension or incomprehension between generations old and young abound, it is logical to look to the past for some clues about the origins of our present dilemmas. Ideally, an historical perspective can identify the directions of change that inform our own society, and the causes of these trends, so that those concerned with remediation can improve their sense of the intensity of current problems and the reasons for them. Even more, history can help us separate essentially inherent diffi-

Peter N. Stearns is Heinz Professor and Head, Department of History, Carnegie Mellon University, Pittsburgh, PA 15213, and Editor of the *Journal of Social History*.

culties in relationships between young and old from those that are specifically rooted in our culture and/or in modern times, the latter presumably being easier to address. Fortunately, considerable historical work on old age in the Western world, developed over the past fifteen years, does provide a framework for this kind of focused historical analysis, though there are still important challenges for research.

THE MODERNIZATION MODEL

Relations between old and young have never been easy in the history of Western civilization, at least since the later Middle Ages. This point is important to stress, since it obviates the notion of an idealized past in contrast to a bleak present. We should, therefore, look to the cause of current dilemmas as emanating from the "forces of modernization."

To be sure, some intergenerational bonds existed that have since declined. Historically, in some illiterate societies, young people undoubtedly imbibed wisdom from the stories told by their elders, but images of the elderly serving as repositories of collective memory are less common in pre-industrial Western history than in some other agricultural societies. Important traces of this function could be found when the young turned to old women to provide folk medicine in cases of childbirth or illness. Christian teachings urged deference to the elderly, and a number of institutions helped drive this home to a younger audience. Church seating in colonial Massachusetts, for example, gave pride of place to those of mature age. There is evidence that young people looked forward to reaching a relatively advanced age as a badge of wisdom and dignity. This at times favored an older appearance (the prevalence of whitened wigs in colonial days) and many people were prone to claim to be older than they actually were (Fischer, 1978).

There is some basis, therefore, in an historical model that emphasizes how the functions of older people on behalf of children or youth, engendered positive relationships. There is also evidence that some of these favorable links would measurably decline with modernization (see Tout, in this edition). Thus in the United States, a passion for youngness developed early in the 19th century that cut into the hallowed character of old age. By the 1820s people, when they lied about their age, lied toward youth, in the pattern that remains with us today. By the later 19th century, old age was increasingly linked with medical infirmity as doctors, in well-publicized reports, probed the inevitable degeneration of the human mind and body (Achenbaum, 1978; Haber, 1983). In an industrial society that stressed energy and the capacity to learn, this revision of the cultural images associated with old age, away from venerability and toward decrepitude, undoubtedly complicated old-young relationships, and unquestionably encouraged a new impatience by youth toward their elders.

But these general cultural patterns are not the whole story, at least in the Western context. For general Western culture did not in fact produce smooth intergenerational relations before the advent of industrial society, nor did industrial standards, despite their youth bias, yield a universal deterioration.

BACKGROUND: THE CENTURIES BEFORE INDUSTRIALIZATION

In the pre-industrial West, and it can be suggested that Western patterns were unusual among agricultural civilizations, the actual contacts between young and old were conditioned by a number of factors besides a respectful culture. In the first place, the demography of Western society mitigated against predictable old-young interaction. While it is not true, as Simone de Beauvoir contended, that an elderly population barely existed before the late 18th century, the size of this population was limited by high death rates and, more important, its overlap with the younger generation was restricted by late average marriage ages outside the wealthy elites. With marriage occurring typically in the later twenties, and an adult life expectancy into the later fifties, it is obvious that relatively few, even first-born children, would have much likelihood of extensive contacts with grandparents. In this respect, Western society differed from other cultures where lower marriage ages, and therefore lower average parent age at first births, prevailed, and where norms for relationships with grandparents had to be built more firmly into family patterns (Stearns, 1982). To be sure, colonial Americans departed from the Western family model to an extent, though more in the 17th century than the 18th, by having lower marriage ages (around 23) and greater adult longevity, but even here a firm set of intergenerational standards did not clearly develop.

Family Tension

What conflicts there were, furthermore, were frequently bedeviled with tension. Well before modern times, Western popular culture stressed the importance of nuclear overextended families, which meant that, upon marriage, parent-child contacts took pride of place over wider relationships including those with any older family members. Contacts with older parents might continue after marriage; in some cases older family members lived in the household, in others in a back house or some other nearby residence. The emphasis, however, was not on the older person's role, certainly not on any venerable dignity. Young children may well have related pleasantly to older relatives who co-resided, an aspect of pre-industrial family history that has not been fleshed out. Tensions between youth and older relatives, often their own aging parents, were frequently acute.

Economic Tensions

The old were seen as taking valuable resources from the family, and giving little or nothing in return. Many older parents, forced by poor health to curtail their work activities in favor of turning all or part of their property over to a young-adult/child, had to draw up detailed contracts even to assure ongoing subsistence in a society that depended primarily on divisions of labor in the nuclear family (among wives, husbands and children) rather than a more extended context. Many young adults, in this setting, indeed waited impatiently for older relatives to die because their own economic independence, their own full adulthood in the sense of marriage opportunities and the like depended on this death for access to the necessary property. Small wonder that many young people repeated general cultural criticisms of the qualities of old age by blasting the presumably characteristic avarice of the elderly, criticizing those old people (particularly women) who showed inclinations to re-marry or display sexual interests, and so on (Thomas, 1976).

Discipline

Some historians would add to this picture of characteristic eco-nomic tensions between young and old as a more purely psycholog-ical dimension. The strict discipline imposed on children by many parents in pre-industrial Western society may have built animosities that, though repressed while parents were in full vigor, could burst forth when old age weakened enforceable authority. It was in this sense no accident that important popular outbursts such as the witchcraft hysteria of the 17th century pitted predominantly young accusers against predominantly old (and usually female) targets. The witchcraft trials certainly reflected the functionlessness of many old people in pre-industrial society in the West, and may in fact have taught older people that their safest course was a low profile, a passivity that would minimize the chance of confrontation with the young.

Property Conflicts

The conflict image should not be overdrawn. Tension normally coexisted with some respect for the presumed wisdom of the old. Conditions in the American colonies, where property was more abundant than in Western Europe, may have minimized contest for many older parents were able to yield some land to their children relatively early on, maintaining cordial relations in the process (Greven, 1970). The fact remains that for a variety of reasons, headed by the demography of the Western-style family, no set posi-tions were assigned to the old in the care of the young, and the old were not readily embraced in the dominant family economic unit. Strong bias against some of the qualities attributed to old age did not await modern times in Western culture, and might strain the actual relationships developed between old and young.

THE IMPACT OF INDUSTRIALIZATION

As Western societies, including the new United States, became increasingly urban and industrial during the 19th century, the channels between young and old may well, in contrast to much conventional wisdom, have become more fruitful and elaborate for many decades. Three developments facilitated new contacts between old and young in a framework where substantial birthrates (which had indeed risen during the 18th century) maintained the elderly as a fairly low percentage of the population total until after about 1900.

1. With new forms of employment, based primarily on getting paying jobs rather than awaiting access to inherited property or position, one of the traditional sources of old-young tension declined. One historian has asserted, with real plausibility though unfortunately not much direct evidence, that relations between young and old were improved in the family context, as controversy over property control declined and childrearing methods began to soften (Fischer, 1978). Certainly the image of the old in families took on new characteristics. Laments about avarice waned in favor of an emphasis on benign grandparenthood. Rosy-cheeked grandmothers cropped up in stories and advertising, dispensing a combination of sound advice and great affection.

2. Co-residence with grandparents increased somewhat. Working-class families were more likely to have an older relative within the household than were their counterparts in the countryside. This in part reflected housing shortages in the growing cities and, by itself, sheds little light on interactions between old and young. However, in some cases the functions of the elderly also increased, while retaining more than small traces of careful economic negotiations. Older people could serve as babysitters, increasingly needed in a society where work was separate from home. (Anderson, 1971).

3. Finally, the old gained some new cultural functions, though rarely without considerable attendant ambivalence. In a rapidly changing social setting, many people viewed the family as a bastion of traditional values, ironically pushing new tasks on

the institution in the process. American society experienced periodic fads for family reunions as a means to compensate for the effects of geographic mobility. Many ethnic groups looked for sources of continuity with the old country. In these contexts, older people could be called upon to undertake new educational roles with the young to mitigate the effects of nonfamilial schooling, media pressures and the like. Here was an area where contacts between young and old might be encouraged not only within families but in larger groups, such as religious, ethnic, and social organizations.

New tensions developed, to be sure. As young people spent increasing amounts of time outside the home and its environs, at work or in school, their time available for interaction with older people diminished. Overall emphasis on the virtues of youth, on new learning over traditional values and techniques, or on new leisure interests such as organized sports could reduce the young's patience with the old even when shared time was available. For a minority of the old, particularly in poor families, a pattern of institutionalization developed in the 19th century that guaranteed increasing generational isolation. Alms houses and certain kinds of hospitals (including mental institutions) housed increasing numbers of elderly whom younger kin could not or would not care for, and generational segregation in such institutions unquestionably increased (Van Tassel & Stearns, 1986).

The first century of industrialization, however, yielded no general sense that relations between old and young constituted a problem. Partly, this was because other issues pressed more keenly, in a society in which the old were easy to ignore. Partly, this resulted from misleadingly nostalgic imagery about beloved grandparents as part of a sentimental approach to family life. The absence of any coherent sense of a deterioration in old-young relations (apart from occasional laments about values conflicts between old-country grandparents and their brash American-schooled descendants) reflects the real possibility that no clear deterioration in fact occurred. The acquisition of some new functions in relation to the young gave older people channels of communication that may have compensated for the undeniable decline in the official veneration accorded the elderly.

THE TWENTIETH CENTURY

A more unambiguous break in old-young relations awaited the middle decades of the 20th century in the United States and Western Europe alike. The key change was residential though it reflected a wider cultural conflict between old and young.

The kinds of older people who, in the 19th century and before, had lived with younger kin began to move out after the 1920s. In 1900, almost 29% of all Americans over 65 lived with another relative other than spouse; by 1980 this figure had dropped to under 10%. Only 4% of the elderly lived with a married child in 1980 in contrast to the 26% rate in 1900. Figures from Western Europe, though slightly more sluggish, moved in similar directions, reflecting a real, society-wide revolution in family structure and a growing separation of older people from the most direct, immediate relationships with younger family members. Remarkably, also, this revolution was accompanied by very little comment, and certainly scant criticism, suggesting that most individuals, old and young alike, found a break in previous intimacy rather natural (Hareven, 1976; Smith, 1981).

The impact of this change, one of the real watersheds in the modern history of old age, need not be exaggerated. Automobiles and telephones allowed frequent contact between old and young even when in separate households. Literally, in some groups, daily interaction, particularly between adult women and their older mothers, occurred. This contact bore less strongly on children and youth, however, and for them older relatives became in many cases a genuinely remote force. Accompanying the residential change, furthermore, was the rise of pension-supported retirements which reduced the dependency of the elderly on younger kin, therefore, facilitating separate households. By curtailing the work roles of older people, yet another contact site between old and young in the workplace was eliminated (Graebner, 1980; Gratton, 1986; Van Tassel & Stearns, 1986).

Why did the literal distance between old and young increase? Growing prosperity and social security measures enabled the change, but they do not explain it. In one sense, the drop in extended households restored elements of the older Western tradition which has emphasized the independence of the nuclear family. This would suggest that despite few widely-articulated signs of tension, the increase in old-young interaction and cohabitation during the industrial revolution decades had been resented by those involved. Not only parents and children, but also the elderly themselves seem to rate independence highly, at real cost to intergenerational contacts and at real risk, at least for many elderly, of outright loneliness.

More modern factors certainly contributed to the break between old and young. A French study suggested that many old people welcomed the chance to escape their progeny because they disliked their peripheral status in the extended family, saw their childrearing advice routinely scorned by young parents eager to be up-to-date and felt harassed by the rude manners and loud music, and this before rock 'n roll, of their adolescent grandchildren (Pacaud & Lahalle, 1969). A society that promoted age-grading, from school days onward, certainly encouraged increased association among one's generational peers, and age-specific subcultures developed to an unprecedented degree, most obviously among the young, but now among many elderly as well. Some, therefore, deliberately selected residences from which young people were excluded save on a visiting basis.

Certainly, the framework set for old-young contacts by the residential revolution, mass schooling and retirement (i.e., the framework that took shape from the 1920s onward) has continued without significant deflection to the present day. The decline of adult control over adolescents after 1945 extended youth's impatience with age. The baby boom years between 1943 and 1963, focusing attention on the young and generating suspicion not just of the old, but of anyone over 30, worked to the same effect. The renewed concern about the growing old-age segment that emerged after the baby-boom's end hardly produced any systematic measures toward re-linking the generations, and some young, resentful of the elderly's visibility, seemed to regard the old primarily as targets for attack, an extreme but not entirely illogical result of the larger trend that had worked toward growing generational gaps.

The picture should not be overdrawn. Separate residence, and some 85% of all older Americans still lived in the same region with at least one younger kin, did not preclude frequent and warm contact. Just as property tensions had earlier receded, so some of the tensions generated by co-residence now declined, leaving the way open for more positive alloyed bonds of affection. Many grandparents developed intense ties with their descendants, and the sentiments were often reciprocated. Concern about family roots and reunions, surfacing again in the 1970s, gave older family members a definite place in the family system and this place served as a point of reference for the young. New patterns of women's work and the growth of single-parent families gave many older people renewed roles as caretakers for the young, particularly in some family subcultures. While polls routinely reflected belief by the elderly that their contacts with the young had deteriorated, not in itself a new theme in human history, few old people reported embittered isolation. Forecast of generational political battles, pitted around entitlements for the old that are paid for by the young, have not materialized as young workers and retirees continue to agree on key social programs if not on all details.

CONCLUSION

The historical record, despite important qualifications, abundantly supports the belief that the relationships between old and young are not only wanting, but in important senses newly wanting. There are less regular and structured interactions between old and young in the later 20th century than ever before. Not only families but also other institutions in modern society have reduced the chance for old and young to share activities in meaningful ways.

The historical record is also complex. There is no magic past, at least in Western culture, to inspire a model for the future. Indeed we must be aware that certain Western values have long inhibited intergenerational contacts; a new effort to create such contacts is not merely countering recent impediments, but some barriers of longer standing. The historical record also suggests, however, the possibility of seeking mutually important functions as a basis for bridges between young and old. Industrial society, generating some new needs for the old in service to the young, encouraged interaction in the 19th century. Elements of this model may be recoverable. Furthermore, increased valuation of affectionate relations within the family, though not always borne out in practice, provides another important modern basis for restructuring contacts. Certain modern trends, in other words, that have reduced outright dependency and rearranged family priorities, can be built upon.

Both young and old, as dependent groups, have some shared concerns in advanced industrial societies such as the United States. As the attention devoted to children declines, given the waning of mother-intensive childrearing, and at the same time costs jeopardize some of this century's social programs for the elderly, it is possible that the two dependent groups may find some new advantages in mutual cooperation. In pre-industrial society, age commanded some esteem if linked to property or power. In industrial society, youth won new prestige, and the elderly became more clearly dependent. In the future now taking shape, both groups may benefit from a new balance in which each can find important functions and derive needed strengths.

REFERENCES

Achenbaum, A. (1978). *Old age in the new land. The American experience since 1790*. Baltimore: Johns Hopkins University Press.

Anderson, M. (1971). *Family structure in nineteenth century Lancashire*. Cambridge: Cambridge University Press.

Fischer, D. H. (1978). *Growing old in America*. New York: Oxford University Press.

Graebner, W. (1980). *A history of retirement: The meaning and function of an American institution, 1885-1978*. New Haven: Yale University Press.

Gratton, B. (1986). *Urban elders: Family, work, and welfare among Boston's aged, 1890-1950*. Philadelphia: Temple University Press.

Greven, P. J., Jr. (1970). *Four generations: Population, land, and family in colonial Andover, Massachusetts*. Ithaca, NY: Cornell University Press.

Haber, C. (1983). *Beyond sixty-five: The dilemma of old age in America's past*. Cambridge: Cambridge University Press.

Hareven, T. (1976). The last stage: Historical adulthood and old age. *Daedalus*, *105*, 13-27.

Pacaud, S. & Lahalle, M. D. (1969). *Attitudes, comportements, opinions des personnes agees dans le cadre de la famille moderne*. Paris: Presses Universitaires.

Smith, D. S. (1981). Historical change in the household structure of the elderly in economically developed societies. In R. W. Fogel et al. (Eds.), *Aging: Stability and change in the family* (pp. 91-114). New York: Academic Press.

Stearns, P. N. (Ed.). (1982). *Old age in pre-industrial society*. New York: Holmes and Meier.

Thomas, K. (1976). Age and authority in early modern England. *Proceedings of the British Academy*, *62*, 205-48.

Van Tassel, D. & Stearns, P. N. (1986). *Old age in a bureaucratic society*. Westport, CT: Greenwood.

Child Development and Intergenerational Programming

Marsha S. Crites, MSW

SUMMARY. This paper explores the connection between child development and intergenerational relationships. The social isolation experienced by today's children as a result of demographic, economic, and social changes and the effect of this isolation on child development are outlined as an overall rationale for intergenerational programming. The discussion focuses on four developmental stages of children from infancy through adolescence. Within each stage, the crucial developmental tasks are described as well as ways in which older adults might foster development at that stage. Examples of current intergenerational programs are highlighted within each stage.

A society that cuts off older people from meaningful contact with children is greatly endangered. In the presence of grandparent and grandchild, past and future merge in the present. We need a human unit in which to think about time (Mead, 1972).

Marsha S. Crites is Associate Director of the Human Resources Division, Center for Improving Mountain Living, Western Carolina University, Cullowhee, NC 28723.

> The Biblical story of the tower of Babel begins with the human family as a unit . . . but . . . the family unit splits apart, differences multiply — in language, skin color, customs . . . As they venture farther from their original places, they are separated by feelings of strangeness, and eventually, hostility . . . Members of the family live in separate worlds. (Critchell, 1980, p. 61)

Wholeness and separation, alienation and return, these are some of the most powerful themes in literature and in the human history it describes. Over and over, we hear the stories of families and societies that suffer estrangement and separation, then strive to restore that sense of being connected to the human community.

This same theme recurs in the study of human development. On the path between infancy and adulthood, a child struggles to feel connected, to feel secure, then pushes for independence and autonomy and once again seeks a way to feel a connection with the family unit.

This paper will explore the connection between human development and intergenerational relationships and programming. The discussion will focus on four developmental stages from infancy through adolescence. Within each stage, crucial developmental tasks will be described as well as ways in which older adults might foster the development of children. Examples of current intergenerational programs, which address each stage of development, will also be described.

Today, our families and our modern industrial society itself face unprecedented separation and segregation. Increasingly, children grow up in tiny, highly mobile families. Almost half of all children born in the United States in the 1980s will spend a part of their childhood in single parent households (Census Bureau of U.S., 1980). Children are less likely than before to live near grandparents and other relatives, and with most mothers now in the work force, fewer adults are available to care for children and provide the kind of activities that nurture child development.

Such households create what James Garbarino calls "empty family microsystems" which are too small to meet a child's developmental needs (Garbarino, 1982, p. 36). Single parent homes, as well as other small nuclear family households, need help to produce a fuller, richer range of roles, activities, and relationships for the child to use in his or her development. Indeed, children who grow up amidst a diverse set of relationships spanning age groups, generations, and backgrounds enjoy a special developmental and social opportunity (Garbarino, 1982, p. 36).

Human development has been defined as "the process by which an individual constructs a picture of the world and acquires tools to live in and with that picture" (Garbarino, 1982, p. 237). But to develop that picture and those tools, an individual needs a support system which provides constant feedback. Our communities must find ways to support the families who support the children.

One necessary but frequently overlooked resource is the availability of adults who are "free from drain"; adults whose energies are not totally consumed by their own responsibilities who can devote time and energy helping and supporting families in need (Collins & Pancoast, 1976). Older adults, especially those in the middle socio-economic class, are frequently the only such adults in the community who can help both in the informal support networks to help struggling families and in the more formal intergenerational efforts designed to support family and school functions.

A DEVELOPMENTAL PERSPECTIVE

This paper will highlight the vast literature available on theories of child development that is built on the pioneering work of several of the recognized leaders in human development. Erik Erikson, Jean Piaget, Laurence Kohlberg, Sigmund Freud, and many others have described in their own ways the stages and tasks which shape human development. Our focus will reflect the work of Erikson and Piaget.

Initially, it is important to define what is meant by the optimal development of a child. Below are five optional developmental goals which provide a framework for considering intergenerational influences (Garbarino & Gilliam, 1980):

1. A positive and accurate self-concept
2. Social and intellectual competence
3. An ability to provide for their own material needs
4. An ability to provide and receive emotional support
5. The acquisition of skills necessary to meet the needs of their children and families

With these developmental characteristics in mind, let us now consider the first years of life.

BIRTH THROUGH AGE THREE

According to Erikson, the central task of the first stage of life is the development of a sense of trust in the primary caregiver and in one's own ability to make things happen (Erikson, 1963). Children who emerge from the first year with a firm sense of trust are those whose parents are loving and who respond consistently and reliably to the child's needs. In the second and third years, the primary task is to develop autonomy or independence. If a child's attempts at walking, grasping, talking and toilet training are carefully guided and met with praise and positive reinforcement, the child learns self-worth and control. But if these same efforts are met with failure or ridicule, the result will be a profound sense of shame and self-doubt (Erikson, 1963).

Piaget called this first stage of life the sensorimotor period, when a baby learns to understand the world by way of his or her senses. A block is how it tastes, feels, and looks as it is pushed along the floor (Piaget & Inhelder, 1969).

Thus, the developmental needs of babies are for sensory stimulation, opportunities to move and interact with objects and people, and positive verbal and physical reinforcement for their efforts. The dismal record of foundling homes early in this century in which one caregiver provided care in a nonstimulating setting for eight or more healthy babies reflects the critical nature of these needs. Between 31% and 90% of babies in these institutional settings died by the end of the first year of life as opposed to babies who survived in a supportive setting (Spitz, 1945).

Edward Zigler, the Yale psychologist who helped start Project Head Start, and other child development specialists agree that no adult should be allowed to care for more than three infants in a child care setting. But only three states now have day care regulations which meet that standard (Kansas, Massachusetts and Maryland), and it is not at all uncommon to find ratios of eight to one (Trotter, 1987).

Clearly, here is an arena in which older adults can play an important role either as volunteers or as paid child care attendants. Older men and women, many of whom are themselves lonely and in need of meaningful roles and physical affection, make excellent infant caregivers and can provide the laps, hugs, stimulation, and tenderloving care that make the critical difference for the thousands of babies in child care settings all over the country.

Gramma's Day Care Center, in Memphis, Tennessee, is an innovative programmatic example which provides infant care while increasing employment opportunities for older workers. When a 1981 United Way priority study determined that there were only 271 licensed infant spaces for approximately 3,000 Shelby County families who needed care, Senior Citizens Services, Inc. opened an infant center. Gramma's is now the largest infant day care center in Tennessee with 140 children enrolled and a waiting list which is equal to the enrollment. Of the 55 employees, 52 are over age 55 and the oldest caregiver is 79. The center is also the first day care center in the nation fully equipped to provide care for children diagnosed as potential victims of sudden infant death syndrome.

Another approach which addresses this stage as well as the next two developmental stages is the use of older adults as parent aides who serve as volunteers with troubled young families to prevent child abuse and neglect. The American Association of Retired Persons tested the use of older adults as home visitors in existing parent aide programs in five United States cities. Parent aides agree to spend at least four hours a week for one year with their assigned parent. As the level of trust in the relationship grows, the aides help parents develop coping and child care skills and personal strength to combat the stresses that can lead to child abuse.

THE PRESCHOOL YEARS, AGES THREE TO SIX

The primary work of children in the preschool years is play. But within even the most unstructured play of children lie a number of developmental tasks which must be accomplished before the school-age years begin. Children understand that they are separate, autonomous beings; they strive to master themselves and their environment. Erikson calls this the age of initiative, an age when a child can actually plan ahead to achieve small goals such as dressing himself or making a clay sculpture. At this age, children develop a strong attachment to the opposite sex parent. However, by age six they will prefer primarily the same sex as playmates and in family relationships.

What can older adults do to foster development at this stage? Recognizing accomplishments, providing many opportunities for success, and modeling cooperation, non-violence, and other pro-social behaviors are critical for development at this stage. When an opposite sex parent is not available to interact with a child, an attempt should be made to find a positive opposite sex role model outside the family. For this reason, it is critical that older men as well as women be involved in intergenerational programming.

Examples of intergenerational programming for preschoolers abound. They range from child care centers in nursing homes and intergenerational Head Start programs to reading programs, such as "Grandparent, Read to Me" which fosters reading readiness skills. In each setting, older adults enable emotional development by widening the circle in which children feel at home.

THE MIDDLE YEARS, AGES SIX TO TWELVE

The middle years are a time for developing social, physical and academic competence. Acceptance from age-mates becomes critical as the child begins to define his or her person from reflections outside the family. Children's penchant for secrets at this age is one of the ways they test and refine the feelings of separateness.

Between the ages of eight and ten, one of the major development tasks is the need to relate to a familial adult model of the same sex.

Between the ages of ten and thirteen, this shifts to the need for identification with an adult model of the same sex but *outside* the home (Briggs, 1975).

These are the years when the conscience develops, and at about age seven the child makes the transition to operational thought (Piaget & Inhelder, 1969). Thus, children at this stage can adopt another person's point of view and consider several aspects of a situation at once (Harris, 1984).

Today's society offers some special challenges for this age group. Fears about missing children, sexual abuse, and physical safety in general permeate their world. Thousands of children under twelve care for themselves and their younger siblings after school while parents work. While many of these children seem to cope with this responsibility, others are frightened and feel abandoned, and still others are victims of abuse or accidents.

In recent years, older people have joined parents and other community leaders to develop viable school-age child care programs. Telephone reassurance programs such as "Grandma, Please" of Uptown Center Hull House in Chicago have been instituted wherein children call older volunteers for help and reassurance in those afternoons when they are home alone.

Another intergenerational response to the need for school-age child care has been developed in rural North Carolina where a program called AgeLink matches older volunteers with children in a variety of school-age child care settings. AgeLink volunteers share a wealth of traditional crafts and games, help with homework, supervise games, and act as caring listeners for children at the end of the day.

Other intergenerational programs address the developmental needs of the middle-years child. Examples include tutoring and mentor programs in schools, Adopt-a-Grandparent Programs at nursing homes or with the homebound elderly, intergenerational art, music, and drama groups, and Foster Grandparent Programs in which elders form special relationships with children in institutions or otherwise at risk (Struntz & Reville, 1985; Thorpe, 1985; Ventura-Merkel & Parks, 1984).

ADOLESCENCE

Rebellion, awkwardness, moodiness, and defiance are the negative words that are often used to describe the adolescent stage of growth, and they are frequently based on myths and a lack of understanding about the developmental process itself.

The major task of adolescence, from the developmental point of view, is disengagement, or a releasing of the powerful attachment to parents in preparation for adulthood. According to Erikson, an intensive search for identity results as rapid body changes and new social roles demand new conceptions of self (Erikson, 1968). This "identity crisis" can be resolved only by trying out new identities with peers and with role models outside the family (Hill, 1980). The adolescent must learn how to develop intimate relations and incorporate sexual activity in appropriate ways. Early adolescent romances are frequently focused not on sexuality but on testing new behaviors and getting feedback from someone close. The normal variation in physical development at this stage causes anxiety for adolescents. There may be a six-year span in physical development between a slowly developing boy and a rapidly developing girl of the same age (Dorman, 1985).

This is an extremely difficult developmental stage. Surprisingly, 80% of all adolescents make it through these years of physical, social, cognitive, and emotional change without pathological symptoms. Approximately the same proportion of adolescents as adults, one in five, show signs of serious disturbance (Offer, Ostrow & Howard, 1981).

How can intergenerational programming address the needs of this age group? It is important to remember that despite their reliance on peers, adolescents both want and need the support of adults who will listen to them, respect them, and care about them. The opportunities are endless, but unfortunately misconceptions which both adolescents and older adults have about each other keep them apart. Whenever the two groups come together, some myth-bashing education at both ends of the spectrum can build trust. Older adults can serve as mentors in teaching career development and technical skills, as advocates for youth who have been abused or who have had encounters with the court system, as tutors for those at risk of out of school, or as special grandparents for teens who become pregnant and face the lonely decisions related to child-bearing.

Adolescents tend to be idealistic and altruistic, but they are usually best prepared to make short- rather than long-term commitments to community service. These needs have been capitalized upon by the innovative Early Adolescent Helper Project developed by Joan Schine at The City University of New York. This program addresses the need for after-school programming for ten- to fifteen-year olds by involving them with senior adults in need of help and socialization.

CONCLUSION

Despite the many glowing reports of successful intergenerational programs, there is a startling lack of research available on the real impact that older adults can make on growth and development (Jantz, Seefeldt, Galpert & Serlock, 1977; Lyons, Newman & Vasudev, 1985; Seefeldt, 1977). Some researchers have described positive changes in children's growth based on reporting by teachers or parents (Newman, 1985; Tice, 1981). In the evaluation studies done by the Foster Grandparent Program, significant changes in juvenile offenders' behavior and self-concept were measured with positive results (ACTION, 1984). In an extensive search of nine data bases, however, there were no valid studies which reveal that older adults, as opposed to younger adults, are making a critical difference in children's development. As intergenerational programs multiply, we must not let our responsibility for careful research go unaddressed (see Cohon, in this edition).

Meanwhile, as a society we must abandon our notion that each family can function as an independent unit. We must realize that for our children to flourish, parents must have access to the social riches of extended family members and their surrogates. Children and child raising must stand at the heart of what we are about as a society (Gargarino, 1982). As Erikson reminds us, happiness for most adults lies in the issue of one's psychological and social investment in the future (Erikson, 1963). Investment in children and in making the world a better place for children, then, is critical for our own happiness as well as for the re-uniting of the human family.

REFERENCES

ACTION, Office of Policy & Planning, Evaluation Division. (1984). *The effect of foster grandparents on juvenile offenders in Georgia youth development centers*. Washington, DC: Author.

Briggs, D.C. (1975). *Your child's self-esteem: The key to life*. New York: Dolphin Books.

Collins, A. & Pancoast, D. (1976). *Natural helping networks*. Washington, DC: National Association of Social Workers.

Critchell, M.K. & Locker, J. (1980). *Lifecraft: A guide to intergenerational sharing of activities*. Ann Arbor, MI: Teaching-Learning Communities.

Dorman, G. (1985). *3:00 to 6:00 p.m.: Planning programs for young adolescents*. Carrboro, NC: University of NC at Chapel Hill, Center for Early Adolescence.

Erikson, E. (1963). *Childhood and society* (2nd ed.). New York: Norton.

Erikson, E. (1968). *Identity: Youth and crisis*. New York: Norton.

Garbarino, J. (1982). *Children and families in the social environment*. Hawthorne, NY: Aldine Publishing.

Garbarino, J. & Gilliam, G. (1980). *Understanding abusive families*. Lexington, MA: Lexington Books.

Harris, J.R. & Liebert, R.M. (1984). *The child*. Englewood Cliffs, NJ: Prentice-Hall.

Hill, J. (1980). *Understanding early adolescence: A framework*. Carrboro, NC: University of NC at Chapel Hill, Center for Early Adolescence.

Jantz, R.K., Seefeldt, C., Galper, A., & Serock, K. (1977, October). Children's attitudes toward the elderly. *Social Education, 141*, 518-523.

Lefstein, L. (1986). *A portrait of young adolescents in the 1980's*. Carrboro, NC; University of NC at Chapel Hill, Center for Early Adolescence.

Lyons, C., Newman, S., & Vasudev, J. (1985). *The impact of a curriculum on aging on elementary school students* (Occasional paper series, report no. 524). Palm Springs, CA: The Elder Press.

Mead, M. (1972). *Blackberry Winter*. New York: Morrow.

Newman, S. (1985). *The impact of intergenerational programs on children's academic and social growth and on older person's life satisfaction*. (Occasional paper series, report no. 514.) Palm Springs, CA: The Elder Press.

Offer, D., Ostrow, E., & Howard, K. (1981). *The adolescent: A psychological self portrait*. New York: Basic Books.

Piaget, J. & Inhelder, B. (1969). *The psychology of the child*. New York: Basic Books.

Seefeldt, C. (1985). The question of contact. In K. Struntz & S. ReVille (Eds.), *Growing together: An intergenerational sourcebook*. Washington, DC: American Association of Retired Persons and Palm Springs, CA: The Elvirita Lewis Foundation.

Seefeldt, C., Jantz, R. Galper, A., & Serock, K. (1977). Children's attitudes toward the elderly: Educational implications. *Educational Gerontology, 2*(3).

Spitz, R. (1945). Hospitalism: An inquiry into the genesis of psychiatric conditioning in early childhood. In D. Fenschel et al. (Eds.), *Psychoanalytic studies of the child* (Vol. 1, pp. 53-74). New York: International University Press.

Struntz, K. & ReVille, S. (Eds.). (1985). *Growing together: An intergenerational sourcebook.* Washington, DC: American Association of Retired Persons and Palm Springs, CA: The Elvirita Lewis Foundation.

Thorpe, K. (Ed.). (1985). *Intergenerational programs: A resource for community renewal.* Madison, WI: Wisconsin Positive Youth Development Initiatives.

Tice, C. (1985). Teaching-learning communities: An investment in learning and wellness. In K. Struntz, & S. ReVille (Eds.), *Growing together: An intergenerational sourcebook.* Washington, DC: American Association of Retired Persons and Palm Springs, CA: The Elvirita Lewis Foundation.

Trotter, R.J. (1987, December). [Interview with Edward Zigler]. Project day care. *Psychology Today*, 32-38.

Ventura-Merkel, C. & Parks, E. (1984). *Intergenerational programs: A catalog of profiles.* Washington, DC: The National Council on the Aging.

PROGRAM RESOURCES (By order of appearance in text)

Gramma's Day Care Center, Senior Citizens Service, 1750 Madison Avenue, Suite 350, Memphis, TN 38104, (901) 726-0211.

American Association of Retired Person's Parent Aide Project, Program Department, 1909 K Street, NW, Washington, DC 20049.

"Grandparent, Read to Me," Lakewood City Schools, 1470 Warren Road, Lakewood, OH 44107, (216) 529-4213.

"Grandma, Please," Upton Center Hull House, 4520 North Beacon, Chicago, IL 60640, (312) 561-3500.

AgeLink, Center for Improving Mountain Living, Western Carolina University, Cullowhee, NC 28723, (704) 227-7492.

Early Adolescent Helper Project, Center for Advanced Study in Education, The City University of New York, 33 West 42nd Street, New York, NY 10036, (212) 719-9066.

Young Adulthood to Old Age: Looking at Intergenerational Possibilities from a Human Development Perspective

Shari ReVille, MA

SUMMARY. This paper considers Erik Erikson's theory of human development from young adulthood to old age and Butler and Lewis' characteristics of old age and discusses how these human development concepts might interface with intergenerational programming. Current intergenerational program models are presented as vehicles to support some of the characteristics and developmental needs of older adults.

In this paper, the author hopes to show that by looking at Erik Erikson's human development theory and at the Butler and Lewis "characteristics of older people," we will see the many ways older people are ideally suited to participate with youth in intergenerational programming. If we choose to look at human development, as Erikson does, as psychosocial (i.e., that the stages of a person's life from birth to death are formed by social influences interacting with a physically and psychologically maturing organism), then positive intergenerational contact may be an especially important facet of healthy mental, emotional, social and spiritual growth.

In considering the role of senior citizens participating in intergenerational programs, several thoughts come to mind when considering adult development, specifically the theories posited by Erikson. In looking at the human being from infancy to very old age, Erikson considers socio-psychological development throughout the entire life cycle. If, in fact, human life does span a contin-

Shari ReVille is Executive Director of the Elvirita Lewis Foundation, Palm Springs, CA 92262-6914.

uum of growth, this author contends that it makes sense to pair the young with the old so that each may learn from the other. Let us consider adult growth and development and how children fit into it. Erikson has divided adult development into three parts (Erikson, 1964).

IMPLICATIONS FOR YOUNG ADULTHOOD

First, he considers young adulthood (ages 20-39) which he describes as the struggle of "intimacy vs. isolation." In this stage, young adults are prepared and willing to unite their identity with others (this can happen only after the tumultuous period of adolescence where a sense of identity is to be achieved). They seek relationships of intimacy, partnerships and affiliations, and they are willing to make sacrifices to develop the necessary strength to fulfill these commitments. Although love is apparent throughout all stages of development, beginning with the love of the infant for his/her mother, the development of true intimacy transpires only after the age of adolescence. Although one's individual identity is maintained in a joint intimacy relationship, one's ego strength is dependent upon the mutual partner who is prepared to share in the rearing of children, and in the productivity and ideology of the relationship. Failure to develop intimacy results in what Erikson labels "isolation," which is characterized by settling for stereotypes, and unfulfilling interpersonal relations.

IMPLICATIONS FOR MIDDLE ADULTHOOD

In middle adulthood (ages 40-59) the conflict of "generativity vs. stagnation" arises. Now, the individual is at the stage where he/she can extend caring to others beyond the "intimate other" relationship, nurturance of the younger generation being the most obvious example of this extended commitment. Such "generativity" results in an enrichment of the individual through an expansion of interests and investments in others. The virtue of care develops during this stage, which is expressed by one's concern for others, by wanting to take care of those who need it, and to share one's knowledge and experience with them. Facts, logic and truths are preserved throughout generations by this passion to teach. Caring and teaching are responsible for the survival of cultures through reiteration of customs, rituals, and legends. According to Erikson, the advancement of every culture owes its progression to those who care enough to instruct and to live exemplary lives. Teaching also instills in humans a vital sense of feeling needed by others, a sense of importance which deters them from becoming too engrossed and absorbed with themselves. During one's lifetime a multitude of experience and knowledge is accumulated such as education, love, vocational experience, philosophy and style of life. All these aspects of "livelihood" must be preserved and protected for they are cherished experiences. The preservation of these experiences is accomplished by transcending or passing them on to others. "Care is the widening concern for what has been generated by love, necessity or accident; it overcomes the ambivalence adhering to irreversible obligations" (Erikson, 1964).

If middle-age is considered to be ages 40-65, then this stage would be an ideal pool from which to draw adult participants for intergenerational programming. Those individuals growing into generativity, whose own grandchildren may live at great distances, can put these feelings of caring and nurturing to work in an intergenerational setting. Obviously, there needs to be intergenerational programs nearby, and they need to be made known to their communities so that middle-aged and older people can know about them. Since intergenerational programming is still fairly new, many adults may not give of themselves to the young as much as they could due to a lack of knowledge about and availability of intergenerational programs.

When generativity is weak or not given expression, the personality regresses, and takes on a sense of impoverishment and stagnation. Individuals who are stagnant may begin to indulge themselves as if they were children and such self-concern may lead to their becoming physical or psychological invalids. If the individual could experience some positive intergenerational contact, then this sad condition could be averted.

IMPLICATIONS FOR LATER ADULTHOOD

Finally, Erikson takes us to the eighth stage of development known as "later adulthood" (over 60) where development focuses on the integration of life's experiences, on embracing these experiences as inevitable aspects of oneself, and on accepting an orderliness in life and death. This stage is described as "integrity vs. despair." Integrity can possibly best be described as a state one reaches after having taken care of things and people, products and ideas, and having adapted to the successes and failures of existence. Through such accomplishments, individuals may reap the benefits of the first eight stages of life, and perceive that their life has some order and meaning within a larger order. According to Erikson there are eight stages of man: trust vs. mistrust, autonomy vs. shame and doubt, initiative vs. guilt, industry vs. inferiority, identity vs. identity confusion, intimacy vs. isolation, generativity vs. stagnation, ego integrity vs. despair. Although a person who has reached a state of integrity is aware of the various life styles of others, he or she preserves with dignity his or her own style of life and defends it from potential threats. This style of life and cultural preservation is referenced as the "patrimony of the soul" (Erikson, 1964). Could a more important role model exist for young children than that of an older adult who has reached the state of integrity?

The essential counterpart of integrity is a certain despair over the vicissitudes of the individual life cycle as well as over social and historical conditions, and the nakedness of existence in the face of death. This despair can exacerbate a feeling that life is meaningless, that the end is near, and a fear of (even a wish for) death. Time is now too short to turn back and attempt alternative styles of life. Wisdom, Erikson says, is the virtue that develops out of the encounter of integrity and despair in the last stage of life. Simple wisdom maintains and conveys the integrity of accumulated experiences of previous years. "Wisdom, then, is detached concern with life itself, in the face of death itself" (Erikson, 1964). Those in the stage of wisdom can represent to younger generations a style of life characterized by a feeling of wholeness and completeness. This feeling of wholeness can counteract the feeling of despair and disgust, and it can demonstrate to younger generations that old age can be something to look forward to rather than to fear or dread (see Nee in this edition).

As much as Erikson's enlightening discussions point to the importance of the young to have contact with the old, Butler and Lewis demonstrate how necessary it is for the old to have contact with the young if they are to stay healthy in mind and spirit. Butler and Lewis went to great lengths to determine "what is healthy aging?" (Butler & Lewis, 1973). One of their most important points is that old people must continue to develop and change in a flexible manner if health is to be promoted and maintained. "The ability of the elderly person to adapt and thrive is contingent on his physical health, his personality, his earlier life experiences and on the societal supports he receives" (Butler & Lewis, 1973). Of course, intergenerational programming could be one of those very important "societal supports." Failure of adaptation at any age or under any circumstances can result in physical or emotional illness. Optimal growth and adaptation can occur all along the life cycle when the individual's strengths and potentials are recognized, reinforced and encouraged by the environment in which he lives. An environment that supports and nurtures the strengths and the potential of individuals at both ends of the continuum, provides opportunities for optimal growth and adaptation for both the young and the old.

In many instances, as one ages, he/she experiences social loss. Mandatory retirement and Social Security regulations put people out of work when many would prefer employment. Income becomes drastically reduced and, in many cases leads to outright poverty. The mobile nuclear family system may create an isolated situation for households of the elderly. Children and grandchildren may live miles away and maintain infrequent contacts. Elderly men may find themselves unprepared for finding life meaningful after retirement, and elderly women, after a lifetime of being wives and mothers, can be emotionally traumatized in widowhood. At present, society provides few supports and little encouragement; individual old people must forge their own roles when and where they can. But times are changing slowly. Information about intergenerational programming is spreading, and programs are developing across the country. In September of 1985, the Administration on Aging (AoA) funded a two-year initiative to encourage intergenerational programming. Twelve foundations (all members of Grantmakers in Aging) collaborated with AoA to create and sustain nine intergenerational programs from New York to Palm Springs, California. The final report on the project to be published in 1988 (The Elvirita Lewis Foundation).

IMPLICATIONS FOR OLDER ADULTS

Let us consider the characteristics of older people and how these characteristics may positively effect, and be effected by, younger generations.

The "Elder" Function. If unhampered and encouraged, this "elder" function takes the form of counseling, guiding, and teaching those who are younger. It is tied to the development of an interconnectedness between the generations. It is important to an older person's sense of self-esteem to be acknowledged by the young as an elder, to have one's life experience seen as interesting and valuable. Foster Grandparents are a wonderful example of this kind of "elder" counseling and nurturing. Foster Grandparents work with children with emotional, learning, and physical problems. They have helped juvenile offenders, victims of child abuse and neglect, those who suffer from mental retardation, the physically handicapped, and children recovering from illness in hospitals. Foster Grandparents often comment how radically their lives changed after entering the program due to increased feelings of self-esteem and the joy experienced from helping children in need (Brummel, 1984; Saltz, 1985).

Change in the Sense of Time. Older people have the opportunity to resolve many fears centering around the issue of time (e.g., inappropriate panicking over being on time or suffering with boredom). While the middle-aged begin to be concerned with the number of years they have left to live, the elderly tend to experience a sense of immediacy, of here and now, of living in the moment. This could be called a sense of "presentness." The elemental things of life (children, plants, nature, human touching both physically and emotionally, color, and shapes) assume greater significance as people sort out the more important from the less important. Old age, because of its natural tendencies, can be a time of emotional and sensory awareness and enjoyment. Is there a better place than an intergenerational child care center, where preschoolers are just learning about the world in which they live, for older people to teach the young and nurture youthful curiosity? At the Elvirita Lewis Intergenerational Child Care Centers in Santa Cruz, South San Francisco, and Palm Springs, both the very young and the very old marvel at the monarch butterflies at Natural Bridges state park, at the kitten who adopted one center's backyard, at the beauty of desert wildflowers growing nearby, at the simple joys of nature in the present moment that both old and young mutually appreciate (Johnson & Siegel, 1980).

Sense of the Life Cycle. Older people experience something that younger people cannot: a personal sense of the entire life cycle. There may also be a greater interest in philosophy, religion, art or literature, a sense of historical perspective, and a capacity to summarize and comment upon one's time as well as one's life. In San Francisco, the Seniors Enriching Educational Roles Project (SEER) exemplifies this capacity of elders to pass on an historical and philosophical perspective to the young. People over 60 from a multitude of professional, social and ethnic backgrounds share their life experiences, skills and interests with students in San Francisco's public schools. Two hundred SEER volunteers age 60-90 work as tutors with learning disabled and non-English speaking students serving as computer science instructors, art and music project leaders, career counselors, library assistants, knitters, chess players, storytellers, career and personal role models, and friends (Siegel, 1985).

Creativity, Curiosity, and Surprise. Creativity does not invariably decline with age. Many persons recognized as being creative have continued their work far into old age. Curiosity and an ability to be surprised are other qualities that are strikingly adaptive. Such qualities are especially attractive to younger people who take heart and hope in them for their old age. (They probably reflect lifelong personality traits and benefits the individual who has integrated them into his/her old age.) Such older people are described as lively, full of life, spry, bright-eyed, and zestful. El Arte de Los Mayores Y Los Jovenes, is a bi-lingual, intergenerational program in Los Angeles and was designed to help junior high Hispanic youth discover and cherish the culture and tradition within themselves and their families through interaction with senior artisans. The older artists provide the students with background information on the art form, its meaning and significance, and most importantly, demonstrate to the young that it is still possible to be creative in old age (Struntz & ReVille, 1985).

Sense of Consummation of Fulfillment in Life. A feeling of satisfaction with one's life "is more common than recognized but not as common as possible" (Butler & Lewis, 1973). It is a quality of serenity and wisdom which derives from resolution of personal conflicts, reviewing one's life and finding it acceptable and gratifying, and viewing death with equanimity. One's life does not have to be a "success" to result in serenity. The latter can come from a feeling of having done one's best, from having met challenge and difficulty, and sometimes from simply having survived against terrible odds. Young offenders in Saugus, Massachusetts have a special opportunity to be matched with older people who exhibit this serenity and wisdom gleaned from throughout a lifetime. The older counselors in the IUE/The Work Connection, Inc. are a courageous and wise group, dedicated to helping youthful offenders serve alternative sentencing with their help. They assist these young men and women to find jobs, become educated, and to stay out of trouble. They provide a shining example of what a complete human being looks like in old age (ReVille, 1987).

CONCLUSION

In summary, as one looks at human development from adulthood on into old age, older people do appear to have qualities that make them the "perfect" mentor, caregiver, teacher, counselor, and friend for younger people. These propensities and abilities can offer tremendous help and encouragement to youth while at the same time the interaction with young people can encourage adaptability, spontaneity, and youthful vigor in the old. It is hoped that intergenerational programming will continue to be established in every community so that intergenerational opportunities will be easily accessible to great numbers of youth and older adults. It appears likely that for healthy human development to occur, there must be cooperation and understanding from both ends of the life cycle continuum!

REFERENCES

Brummel, S. (1984). *Stipend volunteerism*. Palm Springs, CA: The Elder Press.

Butler, R.N., & Lewis, M.I. (1973). *Aging and mental health: Positive psychosocial approaches*. St. Louis: C.V. Mosby Company.

Erikson, E.H. (1963). *Childhood and society*. New York: W.W. Norton.

Erikson, E.H. (1968). *Identity: Youth & crisis*. New York: W.W. Norton.

Erikson, E.H. (1964). *Insights and responsibility*. New York: W.W. Norton.

Erikson, E.H. (1975). *Life history and the historical moment*. New York: W.W. Norton.

Hall, C., & Lindzey, G. (1978). *Theories of personality* (3rd ed.). New York: John Wiley & Sons.

Johnson, S., & Siegel, W. (1980). *Bridging generations: A handbook for intergenerational child care*. Palm Springs, CA: The Elvirita Lewis Foundation, The Elder Press.

Liebert, R., Wicks-Nelson, R., & Kail, R.V. (1986). *Developmental psychology* (4th ed.)., Englewood Cliffs, NJ: Prentice Hall.

ReVille, S. (1987, September). *Quarterly report to the Administration on Aging for the National Public/Private Intergenerational Initiative*. Palm Springs, CA: The Elvirita Lewis Foundation.

Saltz, R. (1985). *Help each other: The U.S. foster grandparent program*. (Occasional paper #516). Palm Springs: The Elder Press.

Siegel, E. (1985). *Intergenerating in San Francisco's public schools*. (Occasional paper #519). Palm Springs, CA: The Elvirita Lewis Foundation, The Elder Press.

Struntz, K., & ReVille, S. (1985). *Growing together: An intergenerational sourcebook*. Washington, DC: American Association of Retired Persons; Palm Springs: The Elvirita Lewis Foundation.

The Hispanic Elderly
and the Intergenerational Family

Marta Sotomayor, PhD

SUMMARY. This paper outlines the demographic and economic realities of the Hispanic population as a whole and the Hispanic elderly particularly. The Hispanic extended, multi-generational family is examined both from the perspective of how the older person benefits and how the leadership by older family members sustains and supports younger family members. The paper concludes that in future generations the pressures of life in the United States on the Hispanic family may cause a breakdown of traditional intergenerational support. What is needed are focused programmatic efforts which support intergenerational interactions that reinforce the close family ties.

POPULATION SIZE AND GROWTH

Hispanics are a heterogenous group comprised of individuals of numerous national origins.* In 1980, the Bureau of the Census conservatively estimated that 9.2% of the total U.S. population was of Hispanic descent. The Hispanic group has grown by over 60% since

---

Marta Sotomayor is President and CEO of the National Hispanic Council on Aging, 2713 Ontario Road, NW, Suite 200, Washington, DC 20009.

*In this paper the terms Latino and Hispanic are used interchangeably.

1970, and increased another 30% since 1980. Hispanics have a growth rate that will double their population every 18 years and is five times higher than the 6% growth rate for the non-Hispanic population. It is projected that by the year 2000, Hispanic Americans will be the fastest growing ethnic/racial group in the United States.

High fertility rates and growing migration from throughout Latin America are the two main factors that lead to such population growth, with immigration being the greater influence (Development Associates, Inc., 1983). During the 1980s legal immigration from Latin America, particularly from Central America and Mexico, increased annually by 35%.

Size of the Latino Elderly Populations

The Hispanic elderly population will grow much more rapidly than the younger population. It is estimated that it will triple between 1982 and 2030. And from 2010 to 2030, the numbers of Hispanic elderly are expected to grow by 125% compared to a 65% growth rate for the total population (Spencer, 1986). The growth of those 85 years and over, now at 6.5%, will quadruple within a quarter of a century. Half of the total population of Hispanic elderly are of Mexican origin with its numbers growing at approximately double the rate of the Hispanic origin population as a whole (Current Population Reports, 1985).

Hispanics can be found in every state of the union with 63% of America's Hispanics residing in the states of California, Texas and New York. Mexican Americans are concentrated in the Southwestern states with 11% living in rural areas; the rest of the population is primarily urban (Bureau of the Census, 1981).

SOME SOCIO-ECONOMIC INDICATORS
OF LATINO POPULATIONS

In general, the income levels of Hispanic families showed a downward trend over the last 10 years. This trend varies from state to state for different age groups and different Hispanic sub-groups such as Cubans and Central Americans. The Bureau of the Census figures for 1982 indicate that 30% of the Mexican Americans remained below the poverty level while poverty declined for other ethnic groups. While the median family income for non-Hispanic families saw an increase of 10% between 1981 and 1986, Hispanic median family income showed no significant change (Center on Budget and Policy Priorities, 1986).

Low income levels and high rates of poverty are linked to the types of occupations which are held by Hispanics. Approximately 25%, about twice the proportion of non-Latinos, are found in blue collar occupations; only 9% are employed in the professional and technical fields. Hispanic men earn only 72 cents for each dollar earned by white men (*El Pregonero*, 1985).

Unemployment rates are high with almost 10% of Latinos age 16 years and older being unemployed. The participation of Latino women in the job market increased in the last decade, but salaries remain low. The Women's Bureau of the Department of Labor reports that in 1985 the unemployment rate among Hispanic women remained about 3.5% above that of other women. Hispanic women supported 810,000 families in 1984, but their incomes in 1983 placed 54% of these households below the poverty level.

Overall, the lives of the Latino elderly are characterized by low educational levels, low salaries, long periods of unemployment and underemployment. They are less likely to accumulate assets and lack retirement assets such as pensions and health insurance. They are more likely to leave the work force earlier and are more dependent on Social Security benefits during retirement years. Thus, Latino elderly are at high risk and vulnerable to conditions associated with poverty. Nearly twice as many Latino elderly men and women are married and living with their spouses than we find among the white population. Almost 97% live in households in the community, with most living with family members; 72% live with at least one younger family member.

DIFFERENCES AND COMMONALITIES AMONG LATINOS

Most Hispanic Americans maintain strong linkages with their national and ethnic/racial identity. This is done through frequent travel, proximity to the border, and through access to the various Spanish Hispanic means of communication such as television and radio as well as reading materials produced in Mexico and other Latin American countries.

A unique feature of the migration pattern found particularly among Mexican and Central American immigrants is the variety of migratory statuses. There is a "circular migration" pattern that appears both among legal aliens and those without documentation resulting in a "culture of migration" or an acceptance of migration as a way of life (Muller and Espenshade, 1985). Thus, the culture gets renewed and revitalized on an almost daily basis on this side of the border, reaffirming its symbols, values, beliefs and customs to pass on to the next generations. A similar pattern appears among Puerto Ricans who travel frequently to the island and/or keep in close contact with other cultural patterns and preferences via a variety of means. Thus, the economic and cultural interdependence and interchanges between Hispanics in this country and those in Latin American countries are difficult to ignore, and will become more so.

There are marked class and ethnic/racial differences among the various Latino groups in the United States. Preference for the Spanish language may be the one common element among all of the groups who have roots in the Hispanic American cultures and who find themselves in the United States for one reason or another. Furthermore, proficiency with the Spanish language might not be the main factor uniting most Hispanic groups, but rather a strong identification with the language and different elements of the culture.

While it is difficult to generalize about salient cultural characteristics applicable to all of the Hispanic sub-population groups, there are certain values and traditions that are common among them such as high reliance on family ties, a strong sense of community and religion.

THE LATINO FAMILY

The family is seen as the most important institution for Latinos regardless of their country of origin, length of residence in the United States, racial and/or ethnic ancestry, social class or religious preference. It is characterized by its intergenerational obligations, interactions, and mutual help. For example, for Hispanic families who lack sufficient funds, income and other resources are pooled to make ends meet.

There is growing recognition that for Latinos, the family is the main source of support during times of crisis and stress, providing emotional comfort and protection from political and economic forces over which they may have little control.

The family has had to play an even more important and meaningful role due to the absence of other reinforcements and supports available and accessible to others in the dominant culture. Conditions associated with poverty and discrimination have had to be mitigated and balanced within the Hispanic culture itself by other positive cultural influences and support provided by institutions such as the family.

There are differences of opinion whether the moral obligation between the generations of the Latino family is a myth, or is in the process of transformation and/or extinction. Available data indicates that at this point in time the nature, extent and quality of familial relationships among the various Latino generations are more characteristic of mutual help and the extended family pattern, at least to a greater degree than that found among dominant population groups (Cantor, 1975; Velez, 1983; Sotomayor and Curiel, 1988).

The Extended Family

Traditionally, the extended family has been defined as a kin system organized along consanguinal rather than conjugal lines and composed of a network of sub-families often residing in the same household (Laslett, 1956).

For Latino families, the intergenerational extended family often includes relationships other than those defined by consanguinal and/or conjugal lines. Members of the different layers of this extended network do not have to reside in the same household, or neighborhood for that matter, to exercise the reciprocal and mutual help functions which characterize it. Multi-generational interactions and transactions are not necessarily dependent on the place of abode or geographical proximity. They can be carried out by the different times and places in the life course of the family; or as they move through a variety of network layers often determined by events intrinsic to the family cycle over time. Thus, in addition to providing economic assistance when needed, this type of network provides a sense of belonging, loyalty and mutual responsibility among the members of the different generations.

THE LATINO ELDERLY AND THE INTERGENERATIONAL FAMILY

Most will agree that the elderly family members, more than any other age group in the Latino intergenerational family network, assume a most important role in the performance of at least three key functions: (a) the socialization process of the younger generations; (b) the provision of emotional support, particularly in times of need and crisis; and (c) the transmission and continuation across the generations of cultural and linguistic points of reference that give meaning and direction to individual family members who find themselves in a hostile environment. It can be argued that the functions ascribed to the Hispanic elderly in the intergenerational family are not necessarily different than those ascribed to families of the general population. However, in the dominant groups such roles and functions have not been so specifically or clearly delineated. The reasons are many, but the following are the most significant: demographic studies of the general population are based on individuals rather than on family events and/or units; the needs of the elderly are often separated from those of the younger generations (Steinglass, 1987); lack of interest in the identification and assessment of circumstances and abilities of individual family members to provide certain types of care and to perform certain functions at different stages of the family's life cycle (Lateva and Heuman, 1982); the failure to acknowledge the fact that families go through different phases and stages in the family's life cycle sometimes characteristic of nuclear families and sometimes characteristic of extended families.

Certainly emphasis on youth-oriented values has supported and reinforced public policies and practice considerations that continue to contribute to the lack of understanding of the roles and functions of the elderly within the intergenerational family. For example,

Supplemental Security Income (SSI) regulations can penalize parents whose children assist them by reducing benefits; and/or by declaring the elderly ineligible for health benefits provided through Medicaid supported by community-based long term care services. Both types of services are crucial to families who care for their relatives.

The result has been a tendency to ignore the fact that there are certain life cycle events that are predominant at an older age, but which have specific antecedents in earlier years. Bearing and rearing of children, marriage of children, later years without children, illness and death are events which by their nature encourage or discourage a certain range and intensity of emotional interaction, involvement and reaction at certain points in the life cycle of Hispanic and other families (Glick, 1957). While some of these events have transitional effects, they can provide clues to the many different ways in which a family, as a system, handles conflict and stress indicating its resilience and adaptability. Similarly, family influence at a given time and age might be stronger and more important at other times.

A CASE STUDY

The following excerpts from a case situation illustrate the interplay of factors that are present in intergenerational family dynamics. This situation illustrates how the strengths of an elderly woman assist in the life cycle of her family and how the family can intervene during vulnerable and stressful situations on her behalf.

Mrs. C. is a Mexican-American widow in her early 90's who migrated to this country in the early 1920s; her five daughters and five stepsons were born in this country. She has resided in a southwestern state since coming to this country. She has four living daughters, twelve grandchildren, six great-grandchildren, one stepson, and one stepdaughter from whom she has four additional grandchildren and five great-grandchildren. In addition to members of her immediate family, there are a number of significant persons, mostly church members, who are active in her daily life. Mrs. C. raised four of her grandchildren and assumed the major responsibility for the full time care of two of them until these children were in their early teens; the other two returned to their parents' home at the end of the work day.

Despite her advanced age, Mrs. C. is in relatively good health. She receives Social Security benefits; she is eligible for Medicaid and Medicare. She does not move as fast as she would like and her daughters and grandchildren worry that she might fall (which she often does) or burn herself at the cooking range. She has consistently refused to give up her independent living arrangements. Some of her daughters are now pressuring her to consider other living arrangements with no success.

Mrs. C. has considerable influence in the lives of her daughters, grandchildren, great-grandchildren, stepchildren, sons- and daughters-in-law, and others in her extended family; she has particularly close bonds with the three grandchildren that she raised. Her family is characterized by a great deal of interaction among the various generations; small groupings form from time to time to cope or deal with different situations and/or events. The clusters may consist of cousins, daughters and their children, or daughters and nephews/nieces, etc. At times groups of "allies" develop among the family members to solve a crisis or to "rescue" a particular family member from a situation. Information about family members is transmitted regularly among all of its members by telephone or by visiting each others' homes.

Crises are usually communicated to Mrs. C. who in turn relays the information to the rest of the family. Individual family members are persuaded and/or influenced by her as to the type of action that is necessary at a given time, place, and on behalf of someone. For example, one of her granddaughters, a young woman, was found by the landlord unconscious in front of her apartment. Mrs. C. was the first person called by the landlord at which time she mobilized a number of family members, including the granddaughter's divorced father (ex-son-in-law), who had been kept informed of the granddaughter's problems by Mrs. C. Through her persuasion, it was agreed that each immediate family member would contribute a monthly amount of money to support the young woman while she sought counseling to deal with apparent alcoholism. Mrs. C. arranged with her older daughter to rent an apartment for the young woman close to her. No one in the extended family seemed to question the decision, the actions taken or the procedure followed to deal with this situation. This strong, resourceful, 93-year-old grandmother played the key role in identifying and coordinating formal and informal support service for her granddaughter.

A different event, taking place at about the same time, illustrates the vulnerability of the same 93-year-old woman and her efforts to mobilize her support system on her own behalf. At the time of this event, Mrs. C. was residing with another daughter who had recently obtained a divorce after 20 years of marriage. This daughter had a son and a daughter. This daughter had recently experienced the marriage of her one daughter who had moved out of town and given birth to her first child. Her son was having difficulties adjusting to his parents' divorce.

Thus, this daughter was experiencing excessive stress associated with a phase in her family's life cycle aggravated by a painful divorce and the need to start her own independent life. This daughter's behavior, which in the past had been characterized as thoughtful, respectful and considerate of her mother had become harsh, impatient and controlling and in many ways abusive. She accused her mother of "gossiping" about her, telling her affairs to the rest of the family, of violating the trust placed in her, of not providing enough moral support, and at the same time of interfering with her freedom. The situation at Mrs. C.'s small apartment had become intolerable for the two women, particularly for Mrs. C. who was beginning to feel the pinch of the added financial burden, the lack of privacy, and the humiliation experienced at the hands of her "disrespectful" daughter.

Mrs. C. felt trapped in a painful situation; angry at herself for not encouraging her daughter to become self-sufficient, and angry at the daughter for the pain she was inflicting. At the same time she felt guilty for wanting her daughter at this difficult time in life out of her home. Mrs. C. complained of feeling ill; she could not eat or sleep and was afraid she might suffer a stroke. Eventually, Mrs. C. communicated with another daughter, who after discussion with the other three sisters, decided that she must be the one to ask her sister to move out of the mother's apartment. Considerable amount of family time was spent among them discussing the need to have the sister move out of the mother's home; she finally moved with a greater understanding of the needs of her elderly mother and of her own needs to initiate a process of self-help and reconstruction.

The Hispanic intergenerational family is a cultural resource that can be mobilized on its own behalf; it is a resource that facilitates the maximum development of the individual's potential and that of the family as a whole. Emphasis given to the development of programs and policies that support the strengthening of the intergenerational family as a unit, rather than specific age groups within the family, would do much to strengthen this particular resource. Without this programmatic support, over time the fragmentation and erosion of those very bonds that have historically facilitated and promoted the well-being and strength of the vulnerable Hispanic aged population will likely increase.

REFERENCES

Cantor, M. (1975). Life space and the social support system of the inner city elderly of New York. *The Gerontologist, 15*(1), 23-34.

Center on Budget and Policy Priorities. (1986). Washington, DC: Author.

Development Associates, Inc. (1983). *Demographic changes and projections of the Hispanic population of the United States, 1950-2000* (pp. 13-17). Unpublished document, Washington, DC.

Glick, P. (1957). *American families*. New York: Wiley.

Laslett, T.R. (1965). *The world we have lost*. London: Methuen.

Lateva, L.S., & Heuman, L.F. (1982). The inadequacy of needs assessment of the elderly. *The Gerontologist, 22*(3), 324-330.

Latinos grow 30% since 1980. (1987, September 14). *Hispanic Link Weekly Report*, pp. 1-3.

Muller, T. & Espenshade, T.J. (1985). *The fourth wave*. Washington, DC: The Urban Institute.

Persistent unemployment: Is there a solution? (1985, August 22). *El Pregonero Nacional*, p.6.

Sotomayor, M., & Curiel, H. (in press). *The Hispanic elderly: A cultural signature*. Edinburg, TX: Pan American University Press.

Spencer, G. (1986). *Projections of the Hispanic population: 1983 to 2080* (Current population reports, series P-25, No. 995). Washington, DC: U.S. Department of Commerce, Bureau of the Census.

Steinglass, M. (1978). The conceptualization of marriage from a systems theory perspective. In T.J. Paolino & S. McCrady (Eds.), *Marriage and marital therapies*. New York: Brunner/Mazel.

U.S. Bureau of the Census. (1984). *Census, ethnic and Spanish statistics: Selected social and economic characteristics of the population by sex and birth of Spanish origin*. Washington, DC: U. S. Government Printing Office.

U.S. Bureau of the Census. (1981). *Current population survey* (Series P-20, No. 400). Washington, DC: U.S. Government Printing Office.

U.S. Bureau of the Census. (1982). *General population characteristics* [U.S. Summary]. Washington DC: U.S. Government Printing Office.

U.S. Bureau of the Census. (1981). *Persons of Spanish origin by state: 1980*. (1980 census supplementary report, PC 30-S1-7). Washington, DC: U.S. Government Printing Office.

U.S. Bureau of the Census. (1981, advance report). *Persons of Spanish Origin in the United Sates: March 1980*. (Current population reports, series P-20, No. 361). Washington, DC: U.S. Government Printing Office.

U.S. Bureau of Labor Statistics. (1987, October 2). Statistics quoted in this 1987 issue of the Hispanic Business Magazine. Statistics available from Washington, DC: U.S. Government Printing Office.

Velez, M.T. (1983). *The social context of mothering: A comparison of Mexican American and Anglo mother-infant interaction patterns*. Unpublished doctoral dissertation, Wright Institute, Los Angeles Graduate School, Los Angeles, CA.

Intergenerational Exchange in Developing Countries

Ken Tout, PhD

SUMMARY. In the developing countries, the most influential modern social change is the "greying" of the population. In these countries, there are variations in the ratio of young people to old and also changes in intergenerational relationships. Modern education in these nations is contributing to undermining the roles and prestige of the less educated elders. The patterns of "greying" that have been rapidly occurring during the past 20 years in the developing countries are the same patterns that slowly occurred during a 200 year period in the developing Western industrial nations. These processes often leave grandparents alone, or grandparents living with grandchildren where the parent generation is absent. This is a largely unresearched field in developing countries and where some successful intergenerational models are beginning to emerge.

The cross-cultural imperative for the development of intergenerational programs is to a large extent determined by present-day trends in the aging populations, the breakdown in the traditional extended family systems, and the reversal of traditional roles of elders and youth. These three trends are modern day phenomena.

The intention of this paper is to point out the modern phenomenal nature of the intergenerational debate and to call attention in particular to the rapid dissolution of the extended family system in developing countries. It will not address societies, which like the Central African Republic, appear still to hover on the threshold of family structural change.

Ken Tout is International Coordinator of HelpAge International and Director for Latin American and Caribbean Help the Aged UK, St. James Walk, London EC1R OBE, England.

THE AGING POPULATION

Following the United Nations World Assembly on Aging held in Vienna in 1982, projections of an aging population have become fairly accessible and familiar to sociologists and demographers. One commentator, Sauvy, has said of demographic aging that "of all contemporary phenomena this is the least doubted, the best measured, the most regular in its effects and the easiest to forecast well ahead, as well as the most influential" (Sauvy, 1948).

When aging is viewed demographically, the factor of "population aging" refers simply to the proportionate relationship of age groups with a greater percentage falling into the higher age brackets and a lesser percentage entering the lower age bands. The aspect which now concerns the sociologist goes beyond a variation in proportions and relates to a projection of huge increases in gross numbers of elderly people unprecedented in human history (Binstock, Chow & Schultz, 1982). These factors are a direct result of dramatic falls in both mortality and fertility rates.

The demographer Myers and others, have noted that the so-called "greying of the population," as it currently affects developing countries, is progressing at a different tempo from that experienced by the now industrialized nations during their periods of similar development. Many of the developing countries have entered the aging process from an initial point of vast existing populations (e.g., China, India, Brazil, Mexico) with total populations considerably higher than those of the Western European countries at the time when their relatively modest total populations moved into a more leisurely aging process during the nineteenth century. The pace of change in today's developing countries is immeasurably higher and is propelled by direct transfer of instant resources, such as prophylactic and curative programs and sophisticated industrial technology from highly developed societies. In the case of Western Europe, and to some extent North America, the change grew organically out of the local culture over a longer period of time (Binstock, Chow & Schultz, 1982).

To recapitulate on data now widely available for the period 1960-2020, the United Nations projects an increase of 322% in the "over

60'' population of the world. In developed nations, the increase will be a modest 160% but in the developing countries it will soar to 489% with regions of Latin America and the Caribbean nearing 700%. This trend will affect all upper age bands. For example, the world population over the age of 80 is forecast to increase from about 34 million in 1980 to approximately 104 million in 2020, again with an increase in some developing regions four times that of developed countries.

Another commentator has stated that the "problem of aging" is no problem . . . with a perversity that is strictly human we insist on regarding the aggregate result of our individual success (longer survival) as a "problem" (Notestein, 1954).

Apart from economic considerations, which affect people of all ages although not necessarily with the same force, there are probably two factors which most contribute to turning the "aggregate result of our individual success" into "the most influential" and problematic of contemporary social phenomena. These are the *social* and *political impacts* of *modern education*, the disruptive effects of *massive migration* and the projected societal effects of AIDS.

THE BREAKDOWN OF TRADITIONAL FAMILY

Rosenmayr of Vienna and Traore of Mali (1986) jointly carried out a study of a traditional African culture during the period 1983-1986. A central finding indicated that the "old man" in such society held a position of highest prestige and authority. The culture operated on a basic principle of seniority whereby prestige and authority were conferred by longevity and blood seniority.

This aspect of traditional cultures has been discovered by Simmons in his epic early survey of pre-industrial tribes where 56 out of 71 tribes had the oldest people serving as chiefs. For many of these tribes, the term "old" or "old man" was either a compliment of the highest order or ascribed to the recipient some aspect of divinity (Simmons, 1945).

MODERN EDUCATION

However, Rosenmayr and Traore (1986) found that modern education was often instrumental in breaking the mold of the traditional structure. Frequently, it was the youth who could travel to centres of education, who could assimilate the technicalities of modern knowledge, and who could acquire the political skills to govern the emergent nations. Even at the most basic primary level, school "evokes individual competition" and challenges the infallibility of the senior.

This view of the adverse effects of modern education, when too hastily applied within a traditional culture, is supported by authoritative voices from Tanzania where education has been seen as sometimes "fostering individualism to the detriment of community ties," and from Cameroon where "traditional values are seen to be eroded by mass media transmission of ideas from greatly differing cultures" (CIGS, 1984).

MIGRATION FACTORS

The effects of mass migration are viewed with pessimism throughout the developing world. One of the most reliable African studies of aging states that "as urban birth and long-distance migration increase in Africa, ties to an ancestral home place are weakening, and urban governments will have to acknowledge the needs of elderly people who have lost such ties" (Lekprnyong, Cyeneye & Peil, 1986). Since 1962, a Ghanaian researcher discovered that 18% of rural households had lost all contact with children who, having obtained some form of education, had migrated to distant towns (Apt, 1983).

A study carried out in the Punjab of India, an area of considerable migration, found that only about 50% of emigrant workers sent remittances home and, in the vast majority of cases, such remittances went to the peer generation or a younger recipient. Very rarely were remittances made to the older generation (Oberai & Singh, 1983).

This writer investigated a sample of 121 old people in a Central American area and discovered that 64 of them were living alone. Of the total 121, no less than 43 had nobody to care for them on a regular basis, neither relatives nor caring visitors (Tout & Tout, 1985). The outcomes of migration can be abandonment or cruelty within the extended family system. This outcome has been observed by many other recent studies which confirm the social and economic hazards associated with increasing longevity (Maxwell & Silverman, 1981).

In the course of welfare and development program work in many countries, this writer has encountered many individual cases of family disintegration or variations on the normal intergenerational pattern. An extreme and moving example was that of a 79-year-old woman encountered during the study already cited. At an age when she might have expected some support and solace from younger members of her family, she was found in a tiny shack caring for nine infant children. The two sets of parents had migrated to the United States in pursuit of the illusory mirage of fortune. Since they had no particular technical skills, they failed to find employment that would bring them a sufficient profit to send aid to the family at home. The old grandmother was left, therefore, with not only the domestic care of the infants but also the responsibility of providing a sufficient income for their maintenance.

A man aged 90, widowed for 23 years and having no surviving relatives, spoke of "loneliness and the way young people treat you . . . they call you all kind of names." From many varying developing cultures came similar comments, like the elderly widow who feels safe only indoors because of "young men looking to rob people in the streets"; an 80-year-old man living on the streets, recently robbed of all his possessions and "too weak and depressed to start all over again"; and the grandmother and three grandchildren begging in the streets rather than going home to a shanty of "cardboard and battered pieces of tin, a shack which was abandoned by another shantytown family as being obsolete." The records appear to be endless and terribly ominous.[1]

Representatives meeting at an African conference contributed information on other factors which frequently exacerbate the trends already mentioned. From Botswana, there came a comment on the further aggravation caused by periodic droughts. From Guinea, there was a report on the increasing tendency of urban women to go out to do paid work, breaking down the traditional domestic pattern of work within the family holding. From Liberia, mention was made of a system by which large industrial companies' workers were placed in camps or residences so that there was no space for the extended family. From Zaire, there was forecast the appearance in some rural areas of a "void through the elimination of the active population" which had emigrated and was no longer available for the task of caring for necessitous elderly (Cigs, 1984).

A recent four country study in Asia and Oceania found that in many places the traditional extended family still functioned reasonably well. However, a sufficient percentage of unsatisfactory conditions emerged to suggest that, unless suitable measures can be conceived and implemented with urgency, the underlying trend of disintegration will soon become a significant factor. In two of the countries surveyed, most of the elderly people interviewed did not see family and friends often enough (60% in Fiji and 58% in Korea). In another two countries, while the majority were in fairly frequent contact with family, a substantial percentage was out of contact (17% in Malaysia and 29% in the Philippines) (Andrews, Esterman, Braunack-Mayer & Rungllie, 1986). Again it was evident to the researchers that far-reaching changes in intergenerational patterns could be imminent.

AIDS

A further potential source of societal disintegration has recently begun to affect the thinking of gerontologists involved in assessing the impact of aging in developing countries. This new danger stems from the rapidly increasing epidemic or pandemic of AIDS. It is already customary to think of the impacts of AIDS as affecting mainly the sexually active generation. The mainly homosexual nature of the disease in some societies obscures a further pernicious effect of AIDS. In some developing countries, the disease is heterosexual in its spread. Again, this would indicate major damage within the sexually active ranks of "parent generation" males and females. Epidemiologically, this is a sustainable point of view. Unfortunately, many countries lack the resources for coping with AIDS in terms of hospice accommodation, monitoring techniques, training for voluntary careers as well as for professional specialists, and social security provisions for survivors.

A scenario now identified by HelpAge International postulates the following series of developments within a family in certain developing societies: one of the partners contracts AIDS; the spouse becomes infected; an unborn infant and possibly another minor of the family are also infected; three of four members of the family are dying; the likely survivor of the household, apart from remaining infants, is the grandmother (who will normally survive longer than her spouse); to the grandmother will fall the sad and difficult duty of nursing dying relatives suffering from a disease which is alien to the culture and whose prognosis and alleviative treatment may be unknown; the grandmother must also care for the remaining infants; she will inevitably have to provide the income for the surviving family; she may also find that her local community is so decimated by the disease that she, with her peers of the grandparent generation, must accept responsibility for the preservation of the entire community until surviving infants come of age to fend for themselves.

This scenario augurs an entire new range of intergenerational behavior structures and patterns which will further contribute to the breakdown, both in the cultural roles of the elder and in the extended family cohesion. To this emerging problem, the more developed countries can contribute from the wealth of their own experience of variations in intergenerational patterns. In many respects, the failures of applied response models in developed societies are of great value to newly developing societies in warning of potential dangers and program pitfalls.

INTERGENERATIONAL APPROACHES IN AGING ISSUES

The differences in reacting to intergenerational problems between the developing and the developed countries is related to their recognition and research into these problems. The intergenerational aspect has been the subject of wide debate in North America and Western Europe as well as in other developed countries. In contrast, the subject was virtually unrecognized in the developing world until the 1982 World Assembly on Aging. In the interim, the pace of debate and research has been slow.

In 1985, the PanAmerican Health Organization (PAHO) produced its "Gerontology Update" as an index of gerontological references to Third World problems of aging. It found about 140 references, of which less than 50 have been issued since the World Assembly on Aging. As a bibliography covering all the aspects of life of all people aged over 60 in many differing countries, cultures and environments, such a list is meager by any academic standards. The PAHO document itself declared that while there has been an increase in generic publications within the various academic and professional disciplines relating to aging, "observations specific to the developing countries are still relatively scarce."

HelpAge International, a non-governmental organization most closely involved in developing countries in the initiation and funding of practical voluntary sector programs for the elderly, has discovered that its preconceived priority for urgent practical welfare programs may have been misplaced. The most urgent priority of all may well be to create an awareness to what in some places is still only an incipient problem, even though it is of lesser importance than the many other economic, political and sociological problems of the day.[2] Unless local communities, as well as national institutions, come fully into the debate and are able to recognize the imminent peril of disintegrating intergenerational structures the response will be intermittent and inadequate.

At the same time in developing countries, there is welcome evidence of reactive pressures and experimental response to the mounting problems. This increases the imperative to make resources available so that the pace of acceleration of response can correspond to the exponential increase in demand for research, planning, training, community mobilization and practical action.

A number of intergenerational pilot projects have pointed the way toward wider strategies for either reinforcing the existing family system while there is still time for identifying surrogate family structure based on the commitment of individuals or communities. Many developing countries have been passing through times of budgetary stringency which has restricted experiments in areas such as government grants or tax concessions for careers within the family or community. Experimental intergenerational methods, therefore, tend to spring from within the non-governmental voluntary constituency.

Under the aegis of HelpAge International it has been possible to fund a small number of pilot projects in Asia, Africa, Latin America and the Caribbean based on the intergenerational sharing of technical skills. Examples would be small workshops where elderly workers share their lifetime's expertise in weaving or pottery with young persons just entering the labour market. In certain areas, these workshops will relate to industries which may have lain dormant due to the import of cheaper, mass-produced items. In the present state of many national economies, the local item produced by labor-intensive methods can now be preferred to the imported product which consumes scarce currency resources. International tourism and interest in distinctive cultures have also restored value to trades which are remembered only by the elders. Such intergenerational workshops both restore the prestige of the elder and afford useful employment prospects to the youth.

Other projects in a number of countries favour a more direct and personalized surrogate system. In countries such as India, Sri Lanka, Kenya and Columbia, HelpAge organizations have successfully mounted school campaigns which give skilled educators the opportunity to talk to school children about the realities of aging. The teaching sessions lead on to action programs, part of which consists in the child being introduced to an old person or persons who have no relative. These sensitive relationships depend on the most simple but essential elements such as the child reading the daily newspaper to the illiterate "grandparent" and possibly encouraging the elder to begin to acquire the rudiments of literacy. In return, the "grandparent" shares with the child a rich store of cultural traditions, memories, songs, dances, games, for which there may be no written tradition. With the help of simple technical aids like tape recorders, such traditions can be captured for posterity. Experience has shown also that at day centres for the elderly the grandparent generation is sometimes more disposed to receive from a sympathetic school pupil or student, rather than from an adult professional, instruction on delicate matters such as personal hygiene and domestic sanitation.[3]

To date such intergenerational experiments can probably be counted by the dozen rather than by the hundred across the developing world, but their apparent success constitutes its own challenge to governments, academics and voluntary groups to respond with urgency to the imperative of probably "the most influential" social change of modern times.

NOTES

1. Cases quoted from confidential reports to HelpAge International, London, 1983-1987.

2. HelpAge International, constituted in 1983, has as its main aim and activity the development and support of national, non-governmental age care organizations especially in developing countries.

3. Further information and advice on innovative programs is available from HelpAge International, St. James's Walk, London, EC1R OBE, the International Federation on Aging, or the UN Aging Unit in Vienna. The XIV Congress of the International Association of Gerontology in Acapulco, Mexico in 1989 also provides a focus for debate.

REFERENCES

Andrews, G., Esterman, A.J., Braunack-Mayer, A. & Rungllie, C. (1986). *Aging in the Western Pacific*. Manila: WHO Regional Office.

Apt, N. (1981/1985). *Aging in Ghana*. Legon, Ghana: University of Ghana.

Binstock, R., Chow, W. & Schultz, J. (Eds.). (1982). *International perspectives on aging population and policy challenges*. New York: United Nations. (UNFPA Policy Development Studies No. 7)

Centre International de Gerontologie Sociale (CIGS). (1984). Report on African Conference organized by CIGS in Dakar. Paris: Author.

Ekpenyong, S., Oyeneye, O. & Peil, M. (1986). Reports on study of elderly Nigerians from the Centre of West African Study. Birmingham, England: University of Birmingham.

Maxwell, R. & Silverman, P. (1981). *Geronticide*. Los Angeles: American Anthropological Association.

Notestein, F. (1954). *Proceedings of the American Philosophic Society, 98*.

Oberai, A. & Manmohan Singh, H. (1983). *Causes and consequences of internal migration: A study in the Indian Punjab*. Geneva: International Labour Organization; New Delhi: Oxford University Press.

Rosenamyr, L. (1986). *More than wisdom—Research and reflection on the position of old age in traditional and changing African society*. Vienna, Austria: University of Vienna.

Sauvy, A. (1948). Social and economic consequences of the aging of Western European countries, *Population Studies*, 2.

Simmons, L. (1945). *The role of the aged in primitive society*. New Haven, CT: Yale University Press.

Statistical data from United Nations Department of International Economic and Social Affairs, various publications.

Tout, K. & Tout, J. (1985). *Perspectives on aging in Belize*. London: HelpAge International.

The Intergenerational Movement: A Social Imperative

David Nee, MBA

SUMMARY. The author addresses four phenomena related to the existence of a social imperative for the current intergenerational movement: fragmentation of American society, political strain within our society, a shortage of people to address key social problems, and the opportunities represented by current programs linking elders and youth. These are discussed in the context of public policy and practice in relationship to a social imperative for intergenerational efforts.

An imperative is an obligatory act, an action not to be evaded. Several powerful reasons suggest we cannot evade the necessity of developing more systematic means of bringing together, once again, the old and the young in the next decade. Forging those means, whether policy program or practice, is what we may call the "intergenerational movement."

There are three chief reasons to urge an "intergenerational movement" in this country:

David Nee is Executive Director, Ittleson Foundation, 645 Madison Avenue, New York, NY 10022.

1. to overcome the social isolation of old and young,
2. to overcome the political and social strain introduced by a divisive debate in the priorities of the federal budget, and
3. to address an abundance of social problems during an impending scarcity of younger people.

SOCIAL ISOLATION

Developments in our American society can lead to increasing isolation for both old and young. It is true that increased longevity means that four and five generation families will become increasingly common. On the other hand, geographic mobility, patterns of divorce and remarriage, and age-segregated housing all suggest that children will not have the ready access to elders that demographic considerations alone might imply. Caregiver surveys indicate that most Americans live within thirty miles of their parents and see them at least once a week. That frequency may suffice to maintain a relationship that is already well bonded between an aging parent and an adult child. It is a reasonable question as to whether that is frequent enough to help a relationship develop between grandparent and grandchild. Certainly, it does not leave room for much spontaneity or facilitate easy and informal changes within families for the old and young. Geographic dispersal and attenuated family bonds make it just that much harder for a child to climb into grandma's lap and have a story read or make a creative mess in grandpa's workshop. Assuming that we think useful and important things do happen or can happen between the generations, we need to find ways to make it happen.

On a large scale, it seems fewer Americans have access to a base of broadly shared, common experiences. In the spring of 1987, I had the opportunity to visit an intergenerational work experience program that placed high school students believed to be at risk of dropping out into part-time jobs at several senior centers in New York City. I sat in with a regular discussion group at the senior center that included both seniors and the young people. I was struck by one gravel-voiced older East Side woman who said that she felt that all kids on the lower East Side faced many opportunities for self-destruction, especially through drugs and premature pregnancy. All in all, she said, children have it much tougher today.

This was a curious thing to say, I thought. I asked the woman "You must have lived through the Depression and World War II. Do you really think that kids now have it harder than then?" The East Sider responded,

> Yes. War time was lonely for us with our husbands away, and we worked hard and we went without things. But I can remember a group of women who used to get together in my kitchen after work each night. We had a lot of laughs. *We always had each other*. But who do the young people have? They face the streets on their own.

I suspect that woman is right and that life is lonelier for young people nowadays, perhaps reflected in higher rates of teen suicide. But, isolation is a fact of life for older people, too, who have the highest rates of suicide. Intergenerational exchange can promote healthy engagement for both parties in the transaction.

Moreover, programs that allow elders to give back to society perform a developmental function too. Isolation is not just a function of frailty. The stereotype of the couch potato indicates a sterile isolation that can lie at the heart of life.

The "knowledge worker" returns home after a hard day and slips a video cassette into the television while heating a frozen meal in the microwave. Such a person, if he or she exists, calls on no one to help or for help. This is a stereotype. Surely, there are people who come home from a day's work to help out in community centers, AIDS programs, Little League or Girl Scouts. However, if Americans are not internally motivated to pursue such opportunities, there has been remarkably little external reinforcement or encouragement to do so.

There is beginning to be an awareness of problems related to the privatizing of experience. Younger people are being exposed to new inducements to become socially involved. Many high schools, public and private, now require graduating senior students to volunteer in community programs. Over a hundred universities, led by Brown and Stanford Universities, have forged a "campus compact" which encourages students to act as volunteers in a broad spectrum of community programs. These programs aim for generic volunteering. Nonetheless, the compact is a good example of a programmatic structure through which some young people will become engaged in the lives of elders in senior centers, nursing homes, at home and in other community groups.

In the absence of other structures through which Americans of one kind of social background can become aware of other people's stories and concerns, intergenerational programs are to be encouraged and emulated. But there is more to be done to articulate programs as a strategy for intergenerational understanding and a network for intergenerational services. Just as young people can help frail elders, well elderly people can be in service to youth.

Perhaps the best way to encourage creative alternatives for the later stage of life is to help redefine this passage into "old age." There are now and will continue to be more people living to older ages than ever before. Most of them will be quite healthy and robust. We have not yet begun to define or acknowledge the potential productive roles that exist for them in this later part of the life cycle.

Erik Erikson sees engagement with others in this time of life as crucial in the development of adults. Erikson suggests adults need to experience guiding the next generation before they can grow to a stage of complete integrity. From this experience, adults develop a faith and believe in humanity. Erikson calls this stage of mature development the period of "generativity" (see ReVille in this edition). Robert Bellah shares a similar vision in the book, *Habits of the Heart*. Bellah states that "the notion of community means a solidarity based on a responsibility to care for others because that is essential to good living."

One way to promote the integrity and potentiality of elders is by expanding the options for creativity available for older people and challenging them to move beyond the golf course or even their immediate family. Programs which encourage involvement in society inspire generativity and productivity in the deepest human sense.

Americans have traditionally valued the right to self-determination and the value of independence. But, that independence is hollow if it does not lead to a productive engagement with society. The capacity for truly independent functioning as a person and a citizen springs from and exists within the supports of family, neighbors, community and nation. Programs which address both personal competence and social cooperation as a complementary approach to an integrated life can benefit all ages (see Moody in this edition).

A wise consumer of these observations would do well to reflect on them in a broader context. What will it mean to live in a society where four generations in a family are common? How will the demographic imperatives of aging interact with other trends toward increased social diversity, toward smaller families, toward single parenting? What will it feel like to be a member of a "senior society"? Who will the elderly be in a decade? What steps can we as citizens take in mid-life to change our future circumstances? What new kinds of supports will be needed in our new society? We cannot know fully, but we do know that yesterday's social structures clearly will not accommodate tomorrow's social problems. Diversity means a greater need for tolerance and communication across the groups. Smaller families and single parents means that the family comes to rely on more external supports, formal and informal. An increasingly mature society is obligated to remember that young people are our future.

SOCIAL STRAIN AND THE FEDERAL BUDGET DEBATE

The politics of the federal budget has dominated and confused the intergenerational issue as the general public comes to know it through the headlines. And what amazing headlines they are. The *Scientific American* tells us that older people are a net beneficiary of government transfer payments and subsidies while younger people are net losers. The *Washington Monthly* tells us with more vulgar eloquence that "the old are ripping us off." Progressive advocates tell us Americans for Generational Equity (AGE) is nothing more than a front for a right-wing attempt to reduce the size of government. AGE spokespeople and their sympathizers reply that many self-styled elder advocates also have a second agenda (i.e., socialized medicine or national health insurance).

The whole controversy seems wrong-headed. True, an increasingly large faction of the federal budget is targeted categorically to people over 65 or in retirement with the percentage creeping up steadily from 24% at the outset of this decade to about 30%. People who believe the old are ripping us off do engage us powerfully with that kind of statistic that leaves out too much, both internal and external to the analysis. The "rip-off" scenario observes that poverty among children is rising while elder poverty is declining. By linking the two observations, we are led to believe that they are related and that dollars targeted for child nutrition programs are diverted to elders. That is simply not so.

Our increased federal deficit is a product of several phenomena. The federal deficit can equally well be explained as reflecting a national desire to expand our military options and resources. Moreover, a significant portion of the categorical funding for "older people" in the federal budget is for retirees of the Federal Civil Service as well as for the military. These developments are bi-partisan. Presidents Carter and Reagan both kept a lid on Federal Civil Service employment, and they both mandated a 3% growth in the military budget. But while the census of federal employees has been kept down, the average benefit paid to a federal retiree went from $2,250 at the outset of the 1970s to about $10,000 in the early 1980s and has continued to rise since.

Recent changes made in the federal system clearly mean that it will not be as dramatically generous to future retirees. But, public sector systems reward their retirees more generously than the private sector, and federal civil service is more generous than the average state or municipal public pension system. The apparent reasoning is that public employees forego greater economic return than in the private sector and, therefore, should be rewarded with security in retirement. The point is this: the "categorical" portion of the federal budget includes social security and military and civil service pensions. And they really *are* entitlements, or legal obligations of the government.

The second internal flaw is that focusing exclusively on the federal budget leaves out the important contributions of state and local government to the welfare of children. These include, for instance, the state's share of Medicaid, state public health programs, state and locally funded school systems, municipally funded clinics, and neighborhood health centers.

Third, the analysis leaves out *private*, especially intrafamilial "transfer payments," which generally flow from the elder to the youngest family member. Typically, parents pay for their off-spring's college, which is often subsidized by a second mortgage on a home they might have bought with help, in turn, from their parents (the grandparents of the college youth). So, while the federal budget may reflect one set of transfers, a larger set suggests that we do not fail to support younger people, at least when families have the wherewithal to do so.

The fourth flaw is that even if elders do benefit more from federal policy than children and youth, the solution to the children's problems is not to impoverish the elderly. We must address the poverty of children, but not by beggaring the elderly. This is the fiscal argument for intergenerational opportunity — intergenerational programs help both children and older people thereby extending the use of the dollar spent.

Finally, however, both sides miss an even larger point. While we must make sure that we do not bankrupt our national wealth, there is more to life than the politics of the federal budget. In fact, the most distressing aspect about the current debate is that it casts the future of the country exclusively in monetary terms. Indeed, along with the increasing privatizing of social experience, its increasing monetizing is also troubling. We would do better to define the obvious components of healthy childhood development, a healthy worklife and a healthy retirement and then working back to appropriate public policy — a life cycle approach to budgeting, if you will.

The intergenerational strain, is there, at least latently. Younger generations generally support the notion of income support for elders, but baby-boomers seem genuinely concerned about whether social security will be there for them. It is in this context that more extreme statements take root. The best way to correct this distorted context is to provide the opportunity for younger people and elders to experience each other at first hand. The best response to the "debate'' is not simply to respond in kind, but, again, to develop social and program structures which unify older and younger people.

LABOR SHORTAGE AND SOCIAL PROBLEMS

More important, but much less globally apparent, is the growing discontinuity between a short supply of people and our abundant social problems. Candidates from both parties have run against a "bloated bureaucracy." All sorts of government workers have been led to believe that they are part of a problem, not a key to solving problems. In the meantime, as Tom Gilmore of the Wharton School puts it, nowadays we "romanticize" the entrepreneur as much as we ever did the Peace Corps activist. Our new myths are about the twenty-six-year-old Wall Street millionaires. "Public service" workers, the teachers, the nurses and the counselors, have been devalued.

We cannot afford to bash the bureaucracy any more. We must turn our attention to the social problems that people were originally hired to help address, and sort out means for them to do it with new kinds of assistance and new roles. Elders, retirees and dislocated middle-aged workers may become important to the delivery of services.

IMPERATIVES

In 1985, for the first time in many years, the number of new entrants to the labor force declined as a result of the baby-bust. The number of young people who now join the work force each year is about one million less than during the baby-boom, a condition which will persist until the end of the century.

A labor shortage is developing rapidly in this country, and there are good reasons to believe it will hit hardest in various "helping" professions: health, education and social services. Moreover, the shortage could not occur at a worse moment because the current temper of the times is so hostile to these roles, typically found in government and non-profit organizations.

We can expect that the private sector will compete hard, with dollars and other inducements, for the most readily employable. We can expect that government and non-profit organizations in the human service sector will be disadvantaged in that competition.

Therefore, we need to draw non-traditional pools of labor into the workforce and to modify our existing social service delivery structures to accommodate the new workers. Recent retirees would be one excellent source of labor to work in human services programs, non-profit organizations or some governmental service roles.

We also must make sure that the younger generation is adequately prepared for a more technically advanced workplace. We cannot afford drop-outs anymore. While it is gratifying that public education is becoming a social priority again, there is a teacher shortage, especially in the sciences. In Georgia, some have addressed the problem by importing science teachers from Germany. In contrast, the New York City Public Schools and the Brookdale Center at Columbia University, with support from the Exxon Corporation, are trying a pilot program to bring retired Columbia faculty to high school science classes. The National Executive Service Corps is developing a similar program on a national scale led by an executive on loan from IBM.

Such programs obviously can be a sensitive issue with public sector unions, and must be planned carefully. Yet one private sector union, the International Union of Electric Workers (IUE) has decided that it is in its best interests to address occupational opportunity for traditionally disenfranchised populations: welfare mothers and offenders. Moreover, IUE engages volunteers from among its own retirees and from the community to assist offenders and hopes to do the same for welfare mothers. The retiree mentor typically is linked to a young offender who would be headed for jail if not in the program. The mentor's role is to befriend the offender, help find jobs and help keep the offender straight. Volunteers initially agree to meet once a week with the young person, but usually meet more frequently. A preliminary evaluation of the program indicates that it is successful in keeping the offenders employed and off the streets. Moreover, the evaluation suggests that the mentors add value to the program. Assigning a teenager an elder mentor seems to be more effective than just hiring a professional counselor.

Family Dynamics, based in the Bedford-Stuyvesant section of Brooklyn, New York, addresses the needs of single-parent families that come to the attention of New York City's Department of Social Services. The families helped usually consist of a young, overwhelmed single mother and two very young children.

Family Dynamics employs stipended community volunteers, usually older women, who have successfully raised families themselves in the same neighborhood. The volunteers as role models are able to help the young mother with basic child care, tips about child-rearing, and even provide "respite" by babysitting occasionally. The mothers report a sense of relief and seem to value their contacts with the volunteer highly. The mother's parenting attitudes also greatly improve.

One of the most touching, but practical intergenerational programs is the "Grandma, Please" program of Chicago where frail elderly people operate a hotline for young latchkey children. Children at home alone who have an emergency or simply a need for reassurance can call the hot-line and be connected immediately to a trained elder counselor.

Note that these programs do in fact confront difficult social problems. These are creative, but relatively small scale programs. The number of elders involved in less exotic, but equally necessary programs is quite large. Nationwide about a million older school volunteers provide direct services to children. These few examples indicate growing creativity in attempts to utilize older volunteers, even frail elders, to solve social problems.

We are faced with a huge challenge. The labor shortage means that we must count each child as a precious part of our national treasure. We cannot afford for young people to go hungry or to drop out of school. The workforce of the future will be increasingly composed of people from ethnic minorities, and we must find ways to educate them soundly and help them gain access to jobs. We have at our hands a huge resource and opportunity: the best educated, best nourished, most economically secure generation of retirees in our history. It scarcely makes sense to let the talents and interests of our elders be idle when so much needs to be done.

A good test of social policy from now on would be to consider whether our proposals allow or encourage elder contributions to solve difficult social problems. One valid moral imperative is to avoid waste. We must learn to open and adapt social structures and human service organizations to retirees and second careerists. Thus, we can prevent a wholesale waste of needlessly idled talent and protect our younger people from wasted lives. Replicated in every community, a network of such programs can create a way for us to realize our common stake, share a common dignity and, yes, solve "difficult social problems."

But, ultimately, for our young people, we are going to have to grapple with the need to make social services respectable again. Voluntary national service in an expanded version of Vista or the Peace Corps would be a start. And, maybe, if we can imagine that elders might want to become part of such a structure, and develop social policy that allows and encourages them to do so, we will really have arrived as a maturing society. The age-integrated society should be able to imagine, design and construct a program of voluntary service that embraces contributions from and service to both old and young.

I started with the example of a woman from the lower East Side because of its universality. The great majority of our elder generations shared the experience of World War II. In talking to veterans and their families at home, we hear of their fear and deprivation. Remarkably, what is striking is that those who survived, like the East Sider, do not regard those as the worst times of their lives. Reading Studs Terkel's extraordinary oral history, *The Good War*, one is struck again and again by the sense of a common sharing of hardship, a sense of contributing to a larger and more important whole.

War is not the only path to a sense of shared national purpose. Intergenerational programs can capture our deep desire for community. In our increasingly fragmented volatile and mobile society, such community is hard to find, and perhaps harder to maintain. Intergenerational programs, well conceived and well implemented, are the micro-structures through which we can each learn how the other half lives.

REFERENCES

American Demographics, Volume 8. (1986, March). Ithaca, NY: American Demographics, Inc.

Bellah, R. (1985). *Habits of the heart.* Berkeley: University of California Press.

Holahan, C. (1987). *Post-retirement adjustment: Effective coping with the stress of aging.* Austin, TX: Hogg Foundation for Mental Health.

Johnston, W. (1987). *Workforce 2000: Work and workers for the 21st century.* Indianapolis: Hudson Institute.

Kingson, E., Hirshorn, A., & Cornman, J. (1986). *Ties that bind: The interdependence of generations.* Cabin John, MD: Seven Locks Press.

Moody, H.R. (1987). *Taking care of young and old: The common stake.* New York: Community Trust.

Nee, M., & Bracco, D.M. (1986). *Grantmaking for the elderly: An analysis of foundation expenditures.* New York: Foundation Center.

Pifer, A., & Bronte, L. (Eds.) (1986). *Our aging society: Paradox and promise.* New York: W.W. Norton.

The Social Policy Implications of Intergenerational Exchange

Eric R. Kingson, PhD

SUMMARY. This paper discusses why there is a growing need for intergenerational programs and approaches to public policy. It suggests they provide some important and unique contributions to contemporary American society. These contributions include responding to challenges emerging from an aging society, by developing productive roles for the aging population, bridging stereotypes associated with age, and promoting understanding between the generations that discourages generational competition. These programs and policies can support families and communities through their involvement in family caregiving and the linking of community agencies.

Intergenerational programs and approaches to policy are increasingly needed. Intergenerational programs bring young and old together to learn from experience, enjoy, and assist each other. Intergenerational approaches to policy examine the impact of social policies across the lives of individuals and generations and they seek to build support for services and programs responding to needs of persons of all ages.

This paper discusses why there is a growing need for intergenerational programs and approaches to social policy:

Eric R. Kingson is Associate Professor at the Boston College Graduate School of Social Work, McGuinn Hall, Chestnut Hill, MA 02167.

This paper draws on ideas presented in *Ties That Bind: The Interdependence of Generations* by Eric R. Kingson, Barbara A. Hirshorn, and John M. Cornman (Cabin John, MD: Seven Locks Press), 1986. The author wishes to acknowledge comments provided by Dr. Regina O'Grady-LeShane, Assistant Professor, Boston College Graduate School of Social Work.

—The interdependence of generations
—The aging of America
—The obligation, and I believe the desire on the part of most, to serve others and participate in the community
—The implications of the changing structure of the family with respect to its ability to provide care
—The stereotyping of intergenerational relations as riddled with competition and conflict over the distribution of scarce resources

AN OUTGROWTH OF THE INTERDEPENDENCE OF GENERATIONS

Within families and within society, the generations interdependently require the constant exchange of resources including income, care, time, knowledge and services. Intergenerational transfers, especially private transfers such as care providers to the young and the disabled elderly in the family and public transfers such as education and Social Security, are an expression of and reinforcement for this interdependence. Over time, individuals and particular cohorts are on both the receiving and giving ends of these transfers. In childhood, we receive more transfers (from families and educational institutions) than we give. As parents and taxpayers, young and middle-aged adults generally give more than they receive. And in the later years, increasingly, we receive resources (e.g., Social Security and care from family members if disabled), but we also often continue to give as caring family members and taxpayers (Kingson, Hirshorn & Cornman, 1986).

Intergenerational programs are an important outgrowth and expression of this interdependence. By bringing young and old together, programs facilitate needed transfers across generations. Some, such as Youth in Service to Elders in Pittsburgh, Pennsylvania, provide youth the opportunity to assist dependent elders, thereby transferring needed services toward the disabled elderly. Others, such as Foster Grandparents, and the Family Friends in Washington, DC, transfer care from elders to dependent children. Still others, such as Mentor Programs at the University of Maryland

and the University of Pittsburgh result in bringing the generations together, and they facilitate the transfer of knowledge and culture.

An understanding of the interdependence of generations also highlights the need for an intergenerational perspective on social policy. A comprehensive social policy ought to focus on the needs of individuals and generations throughout their entire lives because the quality of life for any one age group is affected by policies and services directed toward all age groups, and the well-being of each generation is shaped by policies and services directed to public policy which focus narrowly on the momentary interests of any one age group or generation (Kingson, Hirshorn & Cornman, 1986). Moreover, we ought to apply a policy perspective which examines policy and service interventions in terms of the whole course of life and the needs of all age groups and generations.

ONE RESPONSE TO THE CHALLENGE OF AN AGING SOCIETY

The population of persons age 65 and over is expected to increase rather dramatically, from approximately 29 million persons today to 65 million by 2030. The very old population, those persons 85 and over, are projected to increase the most rapidly among our older population, from approximately 3 million in 1988 to 4.9 million in the year 2000, to 8.6 million in 2030 and to 16 million in the year 2050 (U.S. Bureau of the Census, 1984).

The aging of the large post-World War II baby-boom family, persons born from 1946 through 1965, combined with relative declines in the size of the family which follow, and anticipated increases in life expectancy are resulting in population aging. The median age of the population, estimated today at 32.3 years, is projected to increase to 40.8 years by 2030 (U.S. Bureau of Census, 1984).

The fact that more people are reaching old age and that the quality of life in old age (indeed at every age) has improved during the 20th century are significant societal successes — resulting from century long investments in economic growth, public health, biomedical research, and public policies such as Social Security and education (Kingson, Hirshorn & Cornman, 1986). But, as is often the case, success leads to new challenges (e.g., the growing need for long-term care, the maintenance of social roles for the elderly, maintaining and in some cases improving economic security).

One set of challenges are existential in nature. Individuals and the society, as a whole, need to come to terms with the changes and life choices resulting from aging. Simply adding more years of life is not sufficient. Meaning must be found in those years, regardless of the losses and pain that often accompany them. This meaning must be conveyed to those who follow. Intergenerational programs involving the elderly in giving to the young (e.g., school volunteer programs such as SEER in San Francisco, Intergenerational Programs in Dade County and the Senior Citizen School Volunteer Program in Pittsburgh) can be a source of meaning for some older persons and, at the same time, provide role models for the young in relation to the aging process. Intergenerational programs involving the young in giving to elders (e.g., visits to nursing homes and personal care boarding homes) provide knowledge of one facet of human experience in old age. And, perhaps to their surprise, the young may find some old people who, regardless of much infirmity, still have much to give, an important lesson in the resiliency of the human spirit.

The challenge of the aging society extends to improving the quality of life for all. For example, if today's children are not cared for and provided an opportunity to grow, their chances of experiencing a good life in old age will be greatly reduced. Their ability, likewise, to support the next generation of the elderly, the baby-boomers, will be reduced. Similarly, a report of the Gerontological Society of America observes that

> social structure, social policy, biomedical events, and personal decisions at all points across people's lives can and do influence health status in old age in terms of who reaches old age, longevity in old age, and health related quality of life. (Kingson, Hirshorn & Cornman, 1986)

Thus, an intergenerational approach to public policies which identifies issues across the entire life course (e.g., poverty among children and the need for universal access to health care) is a necessary response to the challenge of the aging society.

A RESPONSE TO THE NEED FOR COMMUNITY

Young and old, and those in-between, have both an obligation and need to be part of a community: assisting others, sharing burdens (including taxation) and reaping the benefits of working with others. The elderly have a special opportunity and obligation to contribute to community institutions because they (a) have a very special relationship to the future, (b) have a unique role as conveyers of culture, and (c) have much leisure. Young people, too, as the report of a conference sponsored by the Aging Society Project of the Carnegie Foundation and the Foundation for Child Development (Mother, 1985) points out, also need the opportunity to use their skills in service to others. Again, intergenerational programs provide such opportunities and an intergenerational approach to public policy highlights the importance of assisting persons of all ages to contribute to the community.

ASSISTING FAMILIES TO PROVIDE CARE

Families are generally the preferred as well as the major source of care for their members, especially young children and the disabled elderly. For example, of the estimated six and six-tenths million elderly persons requiring long-term care services in 1985, about five and one-fifth million received assistance in community settings (Senate Special Committee on Aging, 1985) with the great bulk of assistance being provided by family members, usually women in their roles as spouses, children or siblings (Brody, 1981; Brody, 1985; Cantor & Little, 1985; and Shanas, 1979).

The care-giving functions of the family are under increasing pressure. The numbers of older persons projected to need long-term care are growing, increasing to nine million by the year 2000 and over twelve million by 2020 in one set of estimates published by the Senate Committee on Aging (1985). One-parent households and households in which both parents work are rapidly replacing the "traditional" two-parent household with an employed husband and a wife working in the home. Whereas forty-seven percent of children under age six lived in "traditional" households in 1980, only thirty-three percent are projected to do so by 1990 (House Select Committee on Children, Youth and Families, 1984). Births to unmarried parents and high divorce rates further strain the family's capacity to provide care. Additionally, since it is often daughters and daughters-in-law who provide such assistance, the trends toward smaller families and more women working outside the home means that fewer caregivers will be available for the disabled elderly. Other pressures (e.g., the growing need for community-based care for AIDS patients) may strain the families' care-giving capacities.

Plainly, there is increasing need for adequate child care and after-school care for the children of working parents. Respite services are needed for caregivers of the disabled and even for parents, especially single parents. In short, there is a growing need to underwrite the capacity of the family to do what it generally does so well, provide care.

Intergenerational programs offer one of several important ways of assisting the family. New models, such as developing day care centers for children in nursing homes for the elderly, show promise of providing benefit to children, to their parents, and to nursing home residents. Models involving older persons in providing community-based after-school care and models involving teens in assisting the disabled elderly show similar promise.

A POSITIVE RESPONSE TO THE NOTION OF INTERGENERATIONAL CONFLICT

In recent years, a new stereotype of the elderly as well-off and healthy has replaced the old, and also equally invalid, stereotype of the elderly as weak and poor (Binstock, 1983). Paralleling this, there has been a growing tendency by some to frame issues in terms of competition and conflict between generations over scarce social resources. From this perspective, programs for the elderly are (a) a major cause of the federal deficit, (b) a major cause of the growing poverty among children (elderly programs drain resources from the young), and (c) will place an intolerable burden on younger workers of the future.

The flaws of this argument are discussed in detail in *Ties That Bind: The Interdependence of Generations* (Kingson, Hirshorn & Cornman, 1986). Here, suffice to say, the intergenerational inequity argument is based on stereotypes of the elderly and misunderstandings about the aging society. It is a vehicle for some to attack Social Security and other programs directed primarily at the elderly. Moreover, it presents an invitation for young, old and other groups as well (and their advocates) to compete over the distribution of resources, a competition ultimately serving only the interests of those opposing services and benefits responding to needs of all age groups.

Intergenerational programs provide public policy two very positive ways of turning down this invitation to engage in divisive competition. First, intergenerational programs promote understanding about issues affecting other generations. There is a need for forums that bring all the generations together to discuss important community topics such as school bond issues and maintaining tax bases. Senior centers and school systems ought to sponsor events that educate the elderly about the needs of schools in their communities and which serve to recruit the energies of the elderly. Similarly, youth and young adults need to understand the rationale behind social insurance programs (especially Social Security), why they pay payroll taxes, and the benefits and the issues that will confront them as citizens. Second, programs which bring the generations together in service to each other exemplify that, while tensions between age groups and generations may emerge and ought not to be ignored, it is the strength of the bonds between generations which are most striking.

An intergenerational approach to policy is needed to build bridges across many groups to support programs and legislation of common interest to all ages. The centerpiece of such an approach ought to be the elimination of poverty and guarantees of adequate education, employment, housing and health care. An intergenerational agenda should also be extended to include other important concerns. Certainly all generations have a stake in a clean environment and in reducing the threat to the future posed by excessive defense expenditures and the proliferation of nuclear armaments.

CONCLUSION

Intergenerational programs and approaches to policy are not a quick fix for all that ails us. They can play a role in responding to such critical concerns as the high rate of poverty (twenty percent) among children and the growing need for long-term care services, but often only a subsidiary role. Even so, they provide important ways of building community, responding to new challenges emerging from the aging of America, providing service, developing productive roles and bridging stereotypes associated with age.

Today's children, the young and middle-aged adults of the first part of the 21st century, will play a major role in supporting the retirement of their parents' generation, the baby boomers. As the elderly of the mid-21st century, they will benefit from the programs that support the elderly who went before them. They can benefit also from the knowledge today's elderly, the "pioneers of the aging society," can impart about the value of life at all ages.

REFERENCES

Binstock, R.H. (1983, April). The aged as scapegoats. *The Gerontologist*, *23*(2), pp. 136-143.

Brody, E.M. (1985, February). Parent care as a normative family stress. *The Gerontologist*, *25*(1), pp. 19-29.

Brody, E.M. (1981, October). Women in the middle and family help to older people. *The Gerontologist*, *21*(5), p. 471.

Cantor, M. & Little, V. (1985). Aging and social care. In R. Binstock and E. Shanas (Eds.), *Handbook of aging and the social sciences* (2nd ed.) (p. 753). New York: Van Nostrand Reinhold.

House Select Committee on Children, Youth and Families. (1984, March). *Children, youth and families: 1983, a year end report*. Washington, DC: US Government Printing Office.

Kingson, E., Hirshorn, B. & Cornman, J. (1986). *Ties that bind: The interdependence of generations*. Cabin John, MD: Seven Locks Press.

Mother, I. (1985). *Children and others: Intergenerational relations in an aging society*. Presented at a conference sponsored by the Aging Society Project of the Carnegie Corporation of New York and the Foundation for Child Development. New York: Carnegie Corporation of New York.

Shanas, E. (1979, April). The family as a social support system in old age. *The Gerontologist, 19,* pp. 169-174.

U.S. Bureau of the Census. (1984). *Projections of the Population of the United States, by Age, Sex, and Race: 1983-2080* (series P-25, No. 952). Washington, DC: US Government Printing Office.

U.S. Senate Special Committee on Aging. (1985). *Developments in aging: 1984* (pp. 230-235). Washington, DC: US Government Printing Office.

Intergenerational Programming in Public Policy

Harry R. Moody, PhD
Robert Disch, MA

SUMMARY. This paper offers a rationale for public support on behalf of intergenerational programming that invokes an ideal of citizenship. This rationale is contrasted with the more commonly cited "sentimental" justifications such as promoting life satisfaction, attitude changes and good feelings. Four models intentionally based on the rationale of civic education are presented as exemplars of intergenerational programs that fulfill a public purpose by contributing to vital social issues.

RATIONALE

Why should we promote intergenerational programs that bring together children and old people? Why should such programs have any claim on public resources? These questions may seem preposterous or even deliberately provocative. After all, are not intergenerational

Harry R. Moody is Deputy Director of the Brookdale Center on Aging, 425 East 25th Street, New York, NY 10010. Robert Disch is Director of the Intergenerational Life History Project, Brookdale Center on Aging, Hunter College, 425 East 25th Street, New York, NY 10010.

programs self-evidently a "good thing"? And do not the old and the young, along with ordinary citizens, spontaneously endorse intergenerational programming as a way to bring the age groups together and recreate some of the old-fashioned good feelings of times gone by? Who could possibly be against intergenerational programming?

The best answer to these questions is to acknowledge that, of course, "everyone" is in support of intergenerational programming. But those with experience in this field are likely to acknowledge that support, in the proverbial sense, is "a mile wide and an inch deep." When it comes to tangible public support and, more specifically, public *funding*, intergenerational programs are part of everyone's agenda and no one's budget. Until the public, and public officials, are convinced of the crucial importance of intergenerational programming for essential public purposes, support will not be strong, consistent or enduring.

In this paper, we seek to offer a rationale for public support on behalf of intergenerational programming, a rationale that invokes an ideal of citizenship and is distinctly different from justifications commonly cited for intergenerational programs. To illustrate that rationale, we will offer some examples of successful intergenerational programming that quite intentionally have just such a concept as their basis.

We can summarize the proposed rationale in terms of a fundamental ideal of *citizenship* as a collaborative task within life span development. This ideal means that old and young are joined in a common historical task of shaping the public world and understanding themselves as participants in that world. The old are not to be seen as "disengaged" nor viewed merely as an "interest-group" whose needs can be juxtaposed with the needs of young people. Recent debates about generational equity and threats of competition between young and old have shown the dangers of that point of view.

On the contrary, instead of looking at needs or interests, we prefer to look at obligations and shared duties of citizenships. In our view, both young and old are to be understood as members of an enduring historical community, a public world, existing before their birth and remaining after their departure from the scene. Each stage of the life course (youth, adulthood, old age) has its proper task in transmitting or assimilating the lessons of the past in order to create a better future: in short, to recreate the foundations of the common good. This communitarian rationale is distinct from the philosophy of interest-group liberalism that has characterized age-based advocacy in the past.

Intergenerational programming based on this rationale would understand its purpose ultimately as one of mutual civic education. The best justification for intergenerational programs, we believe, is not to be found in their "sentimental" accomplishments (life satisfaction, attitude change, good feelings, and so·on). Nor is it found in a strategy of "free labor" where underemployed young people or older people are mobilized to provide non-paid services to the other group. Attitude change and exchange of services have their value, but defending intergenerational programs in these terms runs the risk of trivializing them and ignoring the larger political and historical questions posed by America's transition to an aging society.

Prevailing approaches to legitimating intergenerational programs typically take an ostensibly pragmatic but, in fact, unduly narrow approach. For example, it is a common strategy to seek legitimation for intergenerational programs by gathering data showing improved life-satisfaction scores for elderly who participate in the programs; or alternatively, showing attitude change scores (e.g., a reduction in age-stereotypes) for both young and old. Under this first, "scientific" strategy, life-satisfaction or attitude-change are taken to be self-evidently good outcomes. Still another legitimate approach is to show how young people can be enrolled to do chores or provide escort services; or, again, to demonstrate how the elderly can function as volunteer tutors, and so on. This second strategy assimilates intergenerational programs into a human service model of program legitimation.

What is wrong with both these strategies is not that attitude change or concrete services are wrong in themselves. It is rather that these legitimation strategies take for granted an image of people as bundles of needs or attitudes and private satisfactions. Need satisfaction is ultimately quite different from the ideal of common citizenship.

We now proceed to describe four models of intergenerational programs based on the rationale of civic education.

ELDER VOLUNTEERS IN INNER-CITY SCHOOLS

One example of the effort is an intergenerational program designed to involve recent retirees as older volunteers in inner-city schools for an after school program to enhance young children's success in school.

Observers of urban education in the United States recognize that inner-city schools today are in serious crisis. The Carnegie Commission and many other national groups have pointed to deteriorating educational performance among children in these schools. What is called for is comprehensive educational reform as part of broader community renewal to reverse the spread of an impoverished underclass in our cities, a trend that threatens an entire generation of minority children. Critical to this effort is the transmission of social skills and values for school readiness and educational success. These values involve something beyond cognitive skills alone. A sense of personal initiative tied to self-esteem, diligence in attention to detail, and broader social responsibility in the community are also required.

But schools alone are ill-equipped to convey these values by themselves; indeed, they cannot hope to do it without the supporting influence of family, neighborhood, church, and other channels of informal socialization. Character development and the learning of values are not the result of classroom learning alone. A comprehensive approach, ideally, would enlist other groups in the community to reinforce the values of school readiness.

It is precisely here where we confront some special problems and opportunities. Among Black Americans, for example, observers have in recent years reported a dramatic bifurcation between social classes. On the one hand, some middle-class Blacks are able to take advantage of new opportunities for upward mobility; on the other hand, an impoverished underclass is left even further behind. In this situation, intergenerational programs may have a unique contribution to make: for example, by engaging older minority people for volunteer roles in the inner-city schools. Recently retired people represent a segment of the local community that now has the time, the skills, and the commitment to traditional values that could well prove crucial for community renewal efforts. They constitute an untapped resource for moral education and the intergenerational transmission of values.

With this aim in mind, P.S. 92, a public elementary school in Brooklyn, New York, initiated a value-based intergenerational program, titled "They're All My Kids." This project was explicitly designed to draw on older volunteers in the local minority community in order to prepare the next generation of children for success in school and for responsible citizenship. In the Pilot Program, conducted in the spring of 1988, a cadre of ten recently retired community residents was trained to conduct an after school program under the supervision of Dr. James Malone, John Jay College, City University of New York. In the program, groups of twenty kindergarten children met regularly each week with elder volunteers who provided structured extra-curricular activities for the children and served as role models for strengthening the children's school readiness skills and reinforcing values.

In this project, an explicit effort was made to link the school to the surrounding neighborhood community, the Lefferts Manor neighborhood of Brooklyn. In Lefferts Manor, 60% of the middle- and upper-middle-class residents are Black and virtually all the children attending P. S. 92 are from lower income or impoverished families. As a rule, the more affluent families of the neighborhood, regardless of race, send their children to private schools, thus weakening the local constituency of the public schools. Our initial objective was to recruit recent retirees for the values education program. But a larger goal was to begin a process of change in the way the parents and all local residents view the neighborhood school, thus enhancing the accountability of the school to the community even for those residents who do not have children in the school. In such a strategy, recently retired minority residents become the nucleus for community renewal, educational improvement, and the intergenerational transmission of values.

OLDER PEOPLE IN SUPPORT
OF PUBLIC EDUCATION

A different, yet related, model of intergenerational programming on behalf of school improvement is found in Brookline, Massachusetts, which offers a valuable lesson in how intergenerational projects can impact on the larger community. Here the question involves not the transmission of values but the mobilization of older people as a constituency on behalf of children. In Brookline, 20% of the local white population is over age sixty-five while at least a quarter of the children in the local schools are Black or Asian. In Massachusetts, as in other states in recent years, there have been measures to limit property taxes. There is considerable evidence from around the country that older property owners without children in schools are sometimes reluctant to approve taxes for the schools. The division between older property owners and children in need of education sets up a scenario for intergenerational conflict which Brookline was anxious to avoid. Their success in doing so offers lessons for others.

Faced with an ominous demographic and fiscal situation, the Brookline School Superintendent acted aggressively to enlist older people as a new constituency on behalf of the schools. This effort included a campaign of public information, school-based services for older people, and active recruitment of senior citizens as school volunteers. Barriers between school and community, along with barriers between age groups and ethnic groups, were broken down. The public schools were used as sites for serving hot lunches to senior citizens and for other services such as health screening and recreation. Adult education programs were moved to community sites, while unused school buses were made available to older people for shopping during the day and transportation to cultural events in the schools at night. Older people were recruited for tutoring, for teaching English as a second language, and for sharing life experiences with students. The result was that, at a time when tax limitation measures were introduced and approved elsewhere, the older people of Brookline voted strongly to support the public schools.

LIFE STORIES PROJECT

One of the greatest gifts that the old can give to the young is the gift of collective memory: the testimony of historical events transmitted through the words of those who were present. For the frail elderly, this cultivation of reminiscence and life-review may be an activity of the most profound importance and meaning. Both old and young can benefit when they understand how individual lives are bound up with a wider historical world.

Over a two year period the Brookdale Center on Aging of Hunter College conducted a "Life Stories Project" with support from the Isaac H. Tuttle Fund. In this project, high school students were trained in skills necessary to provide friendly visiting and also conduct oral history interviews with the frail homebound elderly. Students participating in the project included many Black and Hispanic teenagers who were matched with largely white clients under the guidance of local aging service organizations.

At first, the Brookdale Center limited its role to training the teenage volunteers in techniques of conducting standard life histories with the elderly. But as Center staff analyzed the interview process in greater depth, they attempted to enrich the experience by adding a component that would raise the teenagers' awareness of how the older peoples' lives were part of a larger public domain: how the lives of the old were intertwined with the lives of the young through a common history.

Since teenagers came to the project knowing very little formal history (some could not accurately identify who John F. Kennedy was), the staff worked with them on historical backgrounds of the elderly to stress such factors as immigration, World War II, and ethnic differences. Whenever possible, Center staff provided similar orientation for the elderly. Gerontologists at the Center gave guidance to the elderly in teaching kids about how historical events had influenced their lives. Almost all the elderly participants were delighted to collaborate in the pursuit of these objectives.

Tangible results of the project for the teenagers included an improvement in the academic skills of writing and interviewing as well as a broader awareness of history as a living process affecting their own lives. For the frail elderly, the work of the teenage volunteers resulted in hundreds of hours of taped interviews, eventually transcribed and edited, to be bound in family history books made available to the older people and their families. For both young and old, what began as a routine program to provide services to the homebound elderly became transformed into a civic education activity enriching lives.

INTERGENERATIONAL URBAN PLANNING

Too often the old and the young are juxtaposed as groups with radically different interests: young people have an interest in the future, while the old, supposedly, belong only to the past. Even well-intentioned programs of reminiscence sometimes unwittingly reinforce the stereotype, but some imaginative programs seek to bring the past and future together on the basis of common mobilization for civic action.

The Long Island City 2000 Project, developed by the Center for Human Environments of the City University of New York Graduate Center, was a demonstration project to promote engagement by youth and senior citizens on community planning issues raised by imminent development of the waterfront region of Long Island City and Astoria in the Borough of Queens in New York City. This region is currently the target of a $1.5 billion redevelopment initiative under public and private sponsorship, an initiative which threatens to drastically transform the local neighborhood and the lives of its residents.

Since March 1987, groups of senior citizens, high school and junior high school age students have been engaged in collaborative learning activities focused on urban planning themes. One event was "Community Mural Day," in which 120 community residents assembled to create colorful murals conveying ideas about alternative futures for the Long Island City waterfront area. Another community event, a "Futures Festival," involved neighborhood residents in the construction of physical models of the neighborhood. These models contained components that could be altered to test the viability of different ideas about community development plans currently under consideration. The model building activities were supervised by a retired local resident who learned his special skills in this field in the military during World War II. In other instances, local retired people came forward with reminiscences about the history of the Long Island City neighborhood and its institutions. By sharing memories of the past, the old and young began a dialogue about how the community might plan its own future. They conducted research on historical and architectural issues, and together they attended local zoning hearings and planning meetings. A study unit reflecting the issues eventually became part of the social studies curriculum in the local schools.

Elders were recruited from senior centers, churches, and other community institutions to talk with kids from a sixth grade class in the local school. The two groups engaged in life-review and interviewing around the community. They conducted neighborhood walking tours together, so the young could learn about the community from the old who lived there; they visited public facilities like the police department, fire department, and senior center. Together they redesigned the community, making drawings, plans, and narrative descriptions about what would improve the community. The results were published in a small anthology that was put together by the children under the guidance of the older people.

What is most interesting about the Long Island City Community Planning Project is its simultaneous temporal perspective: the project is both historical and futuristic at the same time. Older people are engaged for purposes of reminiscence and oral history but also as change agents for future planning. They become, at one and the same time, custodians of past collective memory, and in Marty Knowlton's phrase, "gatekeepers of the future."

CONCLUSION

Intergenerational programming often takes a specific and narrow purpose as its goal: for example, providing a clearly needed service (tutoring, chore services), overcoming age stereotypes, or simply providing companionship and the satisfaction of personal contact between young and old. There is no question that intergenerational programs can accomplish such purposes. But we believe that intergenerational programs have a public importance far greater than these narrow goals. To fulfill that public purpose, intergenerational programs need to be conceived in terms of how they can contribute to vital social issues such as support for public education, urban planning, overcoming racial and ethnic conflict, or insuring opportunity for minorities.

Each of the four model projects described above makes such a contribution to vital public purposes. Values education and oral history activities enrich young people in ways that are as important as the basic skills now seen as so important for national economic competitiveness. Building on reminiscence for collaborative urban planning insures that we will neither forget the lessons of the past nor presume that the old have no interest in a common future. Providing services for the elderly through public school programs helps to build a constituency for children in a period when families with children represent a weaker proportion of the voting age population.

So we come back to the basic question: why should we support intergenerational programs to bring together young people and old people? The best answer is because these programs have benefits that reach beyond the needs and interests of the very young or the very old alone. When intergenerational programs are conceived as vehicles for civic education, they strengthen the sense of being part of a common enterprise, a conviction of the common stake for all generations.

REFERENCES

Kingson, E., Hirshorn, B., & Cornman, J. (1986). *Ties that bind: The interdependence of generations*. Cabin John, MD: Seven Locks Press.

Moody, H.R. (1988). *Abundance of Life: Human development policies for an aging society*. New York: Columbia University Press.

Piter, A. & Bronte, L. (Eds.). (1986). *Our aging society: Paradox and promise*. New York: Norton.

Political Imperative for Intergenerational Programs?

Paul S. Nathanson, JD, MCL

SUMMARY. This article examines whether or not there is a political and/or moral imperative for the creation and maintenance of intergenerational programs. Such programs may offer rewards for both advocates for the elderly and for children. The article takes the position that a political imperative for such programs does exist and that such programs may lead to a questioning of government benefits provided solely on the basis of chronological age.

Is there a political imperative for the creation and maintenance of intergenerational programs?[1] For whom? The elderly? Children? Poor children?

I have not been an expert advocate for children, but I have been very involved in the political process on behalf of the elderly and teach law school classes on the legislative process. If one can assume that strong intergenerational programs would sensitize the elderly and their advocates to the needs of children, it is fair to say there is a political imperative for intergenerational programs from the standpoint of children, especially poor children. The elderly, as a group, and to the extent that one can lump them together as a homogeneous group, can be a most effective ally.[2] I have observed this at the local, state and national level. Children could use a strong coalition with aging advocates acting on their behalf in the political arena.

Whether there is a political imperative from the view of the elderly and their advocates is a totally different question.

Paul S. Nathanson is Director of the Institute of Public Law, University of New Mexico, 117 Stanford NE, Albuquerque, NM 87131.

111

Certainly there is a great deal of current discussion about intergenerational equity and/or intergenerational conflict. In difficult economic times, a zero-sum argument is made to the effect that fixed limited resources are available for human needs programs and that funds which benefit the elderly come out of the mouths of children. We hear of the disproportionate share of the federal budget going to the elderly. We hear of the increasing poverty of children in America and the economic advances for the elderly as a group. The intergenerational income transfer of Social Security is called into question. Some state governors have recently declared it to be the "year" or "decade" of the child, and aging advocates are said to be apprehensive about the impact of such declarations. School bond issues or other educational programs focused on children are allegedly handicapped or cut by elderly voters who have no school age children or awareness of children's needs.

For purposes of our present discussion, it is almost irrelevant which side is right. It would appear that the background and media coverage tends to define a reality separate and apart from the true reality. Does this background create a political imperative for intergenerational programming? If so, what sort of programming is needed and what should the underlying motives and/or philosophy be?

I believe the political case could be made in favor of intergenerational programs for at least two reasons.

First, in the face of increasing talk of intergenerational conflict, it would appear politically expedient for aging organizations to be in the forefront of intergenerational programming. By working on projects with younger generations, the elderly could demonstrate to a world skeptical of the aging agenda a sense of caring for the issues important to children. The elderly would gain access to children and their supporters and they would be able to make the case for their own substantial needs. This might forestall direct attacks on the aging agenda by advocates for children. I view this approach and response as narrow and purely defensive, although it may in fact be the motivation for some aging organizations.[3]

I believe there is another, broader imperative. It is more of a moral than a political imperative. It arises out of the status of the elderly as the "elders of the tribe."[4] In this capacity, the elderly and their advocates have a duty to use their wisdom to lead and guide the society for the betterment of all its members. This has not traditionally been the position taken by many aging organizations and their advocates (except for the Gray Panthers and other isolated examples); but in my view, the time is right for such moral leadership from the organized aging community.

I believe today it is morally and politically correct for aging organizations and their advocates to use their political power on behalf of all disenfranchised and needy in our society. Beside being a moral mandate, I also believe it is the correct political position at this time. In other words, it is in the political self-interest of aging organizations to be in the forefront in advocating for benefits to go to other generations. Therefore, intergenerational programs which focus on joint advocacy efforts for young and old should be given greater emphasis.[5]

This broader, and I would argue more commendable, imperative would arise out of an assessment of the proper role of the strong aging advocacy machine in the social agenda of the day. How much should advocates for the elderly be involved in the needs of the non-elderly? There may not be such an imperative now, but it might arise after strong creative intergenerational programs have had the opportunity to educate aging organizations and their advocates to the needs of other age segments of society, particularly children. This awareness, fostered by intergenerational programs, might force the elderly to begin to look beyond chronological age as a way of distributing the benefits of society. This focus on the needs of others could result in aging organizations examining *in public* some of the basic tenets of their past political agenda. Thus, should benefits of society and its social programs be distributed based on chronological age or on need regardless of age? Should some sort of a means test for benefits and services be utilized? Is it fair to demand benefits based on chronological age while at the same time denying detriments (age discrimination) resulting from chronological age? Should society spend more of its limited resources on non-needy elderly or on needy children? These are the very tough questions which I believe will be raised to a new level of discussion if strong, broad-based, intergenerational programs are carried out.

In summary, I believe children and their advocates have a clear political need for a variety of intergenerational programs. Child advocates would be able to make older people and their organizations more aware of the needs of children so that joint advocacy efforts could be launched to address those needs.

Aging organizations could benefit politically from a broad range of intergenerational programs. This is so because they could educate children and their advocates and the general public about the needs and abilities of older people and thus increase and strengthen support for programs benefiting and utilizing the skills and experience of the elderly.

Finally, I believe there is a moral and political imperative for intergenerational advocacy programs in which the "elders of the tribe" provide leadership and support for issues and concerns of society as a whole—especially its children.

REFERENCE NOTES

1. I am speaking only of political imperatives in this discussion and specifically do not address sociological or other benefits of intergenerational programs.

2. Oftentimes, politicians perceive the elderly as a single united force; thus, their effect as a political group may be stronger than their heterogeneity would lead one to expect.

3. To the extent that projects and coalitions are created which actually bring resources to benefit kids, this would, of course, be commendable.

4. Maggie Kuhn, founder of the Gray Panthers has spoken of this role. The Gray Panthers have been in the forefront over the years in speaking of the commonality of concerns between young and old in our society.

5. I have been involved in creating just such an advocacy program in high schools around the country. The elderly and students are learning advocacy skills and joining forces to address the needs of each group. Thus, for example, the elderly are helping teenage mothers with child care while in high school.

BIBLIOGRAPHY

King, J. (1986, April 14). The war between the generations. *Newsweek*, p.8.
Moody, H.R. (1985, winter). Ethics and aging. *Generations, 10*(2), pp. 5-9.
Neugarten, B.L., & Neugarten, D.A. (1986, winter). Age in the aging society. *Daedalus, 115*(1), pp. 31-49.
Taylor, P. (1986, January 20). Remember the generation gap? We ain't seen nothing yet. *Washington Post* (national weekly edition), p. 23.

PART II: STRATEGIES

Introduction

Having determined the imperatives that undergird the notion of intergenerational programs, it is important to become aware of the theoretical framework and practical elements that are the bases of these programs. Part II presents papers that describe the theory and structure inherent in intergenerational programs and addresses a variety of practical and philosophical conditions that are the foundations from which successful programming can emerge.

Steven W. Brummel in "Developing An Intergenerational Program" offers an overview of the elements needed to implement a successful intergenerational program. In addition to examining the technical aspects of creating and maintaining an effective program, he stresses the importance of bringing intergenerational programming and exchange into national focus.

A basic element of program development that many programmers regard as essential for successful intergenerational programs is training. In "Training and Education for Intergenerational Activities: An Agenda for the Future," Karen Vander Ven presents a variety of issues that justify the introduction of thoughtful and consistent ongoing training and education for personnel in intergenerational programs.

In their paper "Evaluation of Intergenerational Programs: Why and How" Kathleen Bocian and Sally Newman review the evaluation components and procedures to be considered in order to collect the solid data needed to verify and validate the worth of intergenerational programs.

With the explosion of intergenerational programs within the Human Service delivery system, we see a variety of approaches to program development. Nancy Z. Henkin and Sandra W. Sweeney describe a systems approach to program development in "Linking Systems: A Systems Approach to Intergenerational Programming" that involves a structured way of thinking about program development and problem solving.

Successful intergenerational programs are the result of effective programming and evaluation strategies. In their paper "Exemplary Intergenerational Programs" Catherine Ventura-Merkel, David S. Liedermann and Jack Ossofsky describe the characteristics inherent in the development of several exemplary programs that contributed to their success. These characteristics include: addressing major social issues, rebuilding natural helping relationships, being mutually supportive to all generations involved, optimum use of financial resources, building on existing services, and opening opportunities for local innovations.

Sally Newman, PhD
Steven W. Brummel, MA

Developing an Intergenerational Program

Steven W. Brummel, MA

SUMMARY. In this paper, the author describes in some detail the following steps in the development of an intergenerational program: needs assessment, planning, implementation, assuring longevity, and supporting a national focus. Inherent in each of these steps is an articulated reminder that thoughtful program development needs to consider, at all stages of development, opportunities for building positive self-esteem among the younger and older participants in the program.

The thoughts of youth are bright lights that shine forth like the meteors that are brilliant in the sky, but the wisdom of age is like the fixed stars that shine so unchanging that the sailor can depend upon them to steer his course.

> The Richest Man in Babylon
> *George Classon*

This paper will consider not only the "how-to's" of developing an intergenerational program, but it will also consider the necessary steps to assure longevity. It will also discuss the importance of bringing the intergenerational movement to the attention of the decision makers at the state and national levels in Washington, DC, and in state capitols. Finally, although intergenerational programming is only in its infancy at this point in its development, it is this author's contention that with proper local development, implementation and the building of a national focus, intergenerational programming may become the preferred way to serve both the elderly and the young and to provide opportunities for each to serve the

---

Steven W. Brummel is President, Elvirita Lewis Foundation, 255 North El Cielo Road, Palm Springs, CA 92262.

other. Given the current financial constraints on government and other funding sources, intergenerational programming may prove to be socially beneficial to both age groups, and cost effective to agencies and systems.

PROGRAM DEVELOPMENT

Before we discuss program development, let us consider what a program is. According to Vickery (Vickery, 1972), a program is more than the scheduled activities for the population served. In looking at programs for older people Vickery (1972) said:

> Program is the planning of activities and the interaction that takes place among individuals when they participate in them. Activities, however enjoyable, have little value in helping individuals cope with persistent feelings of loneliness, uselessness, and depression. Programs are primarily important because they provide the settings in which members may experience acceptance by others, the feeling of belonging to a group, and recognition as individuals of worth. Such feelings strengthen the older adult's self-image and help him feel good about himself. Program then is not only *what* happens and *when* it happens, but *what meaning* it has for each member as he participates. (Vickery, 1972)

This concept is especially important when developing an intergenerational program. *What meaning* will this program have for the participants? Is the program an intergenerationally workable one? Does it operate on the premise that both the older and younger participants are capable of being productive and active contributors? If so, many possibilities are created for many meaningful contacts within the program, not just those listed in the plan of activities.

Intergenerational programming is particularly complicated because we are working with two and often three or more different age groups, each with its own unique needs and preferences. Therefore, activities, delivery of service, formal and informal interactions of elders, young people, staff and the parents of the children/youth, must all be considered in the design and implementation of quality intergenerational programs. Thoughtful development of programs requires these considerations so that all potential opportunities for positive esteem-building are included.

Keeping this in mind, what are the steps in developing an intergenerational program? Based on the ideas presented above, successful intergenerational programs need to incorporate these developmental steps: needs assessment, planning, implementation, assuring longevity and supporting national focus.

NEEDS ASSESSMENT

First, as in every program start-up, it is essential to determine a community's needs that could be met by the program. There are a variety of strategies that can be employed to access this information. These include:

— sending questionnaires to community agencies
— interviewing key community leaders
— conducting group meetings to determine major community problems of gaps in service
— reviewing the research that describes the particular needs of the populations you wish to work with.

The type of information gathered will vary according to the scope of the project. Understanding the *demographics* of specific geographic areas, identifying *lead agencies* serving children, youth, and the elderly, determining if there already exist *formal procedures* for bringing together diverse agencies, looking for opportunities to form a committee or task force to create a supportive local agency council or informal network, and determining what *gaps* exist in terms of services to youth and the elderly are among the tasks involved in conducting a needs assessment. Although this process may be time-consuming, an intergenerational program which is realistically needs-based has greater likelihood of being developed and incorporated into the existing network.

A needs assessment also should review current solutions available or state of the art of existing programs around the country that address the needs identified by the creators of a particular intergenerational program. The wheel is not in need of more inventors; many elements that could be key components of a new program already exist. Knowledge of these elements is crucial to quality programming.

PLANNING

Secondly, program planning must be done. As an outcome of the needs assessment, it will be possible to determine the kind(s) of program(s) which would be most appropriate for the community involved. It is this author's view that intergenerational programs must be designed to support the capacities and potentials of older adults and youth and their ability to function both themselves, for each other's, and for the community's welfare. Only with such planning will older people, especially, have a sense of security and of being a part of the total community. Some of the basic steps to be considered in planning intergenerational programs include setting goals, gaining administrative approval, developing written implementation and evaluation plans.

1. At this point, if not before, it is vital to the success of the program to bring a strong leader on board. An individual is needed who is committed to the success of the program, willing to fight for it, willing to work hard for it, and willing to weather the storms surrounding a new program.

2. Of equal importance is "coalition-building," that is, bringing potential "allies" together in a programmatic effort. Many times an agency or organization would be interested in seeing your program in the community and would be willing to do something to see it happen such as offering public relations assistance, placing a phone call to a key individual, providing advice, sharing equipment or knowledge.

Although it may appear at times that there is competition and fighting between agencies over funding dollars, coalition building can and does occur and when it does, it creates a stronger base for program building. A program's chances for garnering respect and recognition are often enhanced by helping another organization achieve its goals, by commending its good works, and by inviting participation in projects or events with your organization. Bringing agencies together as collaborators may involve forming a task force or advisory council of interested people and including (in a leadership position) the program directors of the collaborating agencies. It is crucial that all planning be done jointly so that the needs of the youth, the elderly and the agencies that serve them are all considered. The greatest chance for the success of an intergenerational program occurs when there is a planned or serendipitous juxtaposition of goals that meet the needs of all the participants. It appears that the potential for such juxtaposition is greater in intergenerational programs than in programs working with only one population group. The human relations that occur when a child or youth helps or is helped by an elder, are full of warmth, understanding, sharing and caring. It must be remembered that intergenerational programs are really recreating "multi-generational families," creating a place for the "soft touch" that is probably more important than the social service being offered. As John Naisbitt said in his book, *Megatrends* (Naisbitt, 1982):

> The need for compensatory "high touch" is everywhere. The more "high tech" is used in our society, the more we will want to create "high touch" environments intergenerational programs with soft edges balancing the hard edges of technology.

3. Naturally, fund raising is a crucial part of most programs' survival. When starting a program, one is in the awkward position of needing funds to get started, yet no one wants to give money to a project that is not known. Here leadership and coalitions can be helpful. A strong individual can convince potential funders of the importance of the project and refer them to allies for "character references." Allies might also contribute a little seed money or engage in joint or cooperative fund raising or grant writing.

4. Goals and objectives are extremely important. First, funders will want to look at them, as will any participating agencies. Clear, realistic goals and objectives simply facilitate implementation. Tice and Warren have identified some important goals for intergenerational programs (Tice, 1988):

a. Establish a sense of continuity that is often lost as families face change through technological development and increased mobility.
b. Create a basis of understanding that diminishes fears of one age group about another. Youth can develop realistic views of aging that diminish fears and negative attitudes. Older people can develop positive feelings about youth.
c. Increase self-esteem and usefulness for all age groups involved. The elderly's experience and expertise are valued for their time-tested effectiveness, and the insights of the young are valued by older people as a means to stay in touch with an increasingly complex world.
d. Create program activities which promote physical and mental health for all participants.
e. Provide services for all ages using volunteer assistance. Youth can provide much help and encouragement to older adults who live alone or are in long-term care facilities. Older adults can be of help in schools and other agencies serving children and youth.
f. Create opportunities for lifelong learning at every stage of development.

5. It is important to gain administrative approval from the lead agencies and institutions involved in the project. Problems can be avoided if there is a formal endorsement of the program from the beginning, and there are key agency decision makers supporting the project during the entire planning process.

6. Before initiating any of the formal steps in program development prepare a written plan of procedures and activities. Create phases with stopping points for examining results such as achievement of goals and objectives and the status of relationships among agencies. Complete each phase before progressing to the next one. It is helpful to illustrate these stopping points on a written time line.

7. The success of many intergenerational programs is often related to the effectiveness of the relationship among the collaborating agencies; therefore, define their roles and responsibilities at the program's inception. Clarify the nature of the relationship among programs through an informal written statement or a formal memo-

randum of understanding. The roles of both the agency administrators and program developers need to be clearly delineated.

8. Retain flexibility throughout the process. Be willing to change approaches as new information is learned in each phase. Seek a self-correcting or internally modifying approach paying attention to what works. Do not "flog a dead horse" by pushing for a particular solution. Be willing to re-examine focuses, emphasis, and organizational structure on an ongoing basis. Many programs fail because there is too much rigidity and there are too many detailed rules. Leaders need to be flexible and open to seeing solutions that "work better" as their program progresses.

IMPLEMENTATION

There are some basic steps involved in the implementation of intergenerational programs. These include: (a) facility and site procurement; (b) recruitment, public relations and outreach; (c) orientation and training; (d) maintenance and support; and (e) evaluation (see Bocian & Newman in this edition). The scheduling of these steps and the identification of person(s) responsible for completing them should be determined before program implementation begins.

Facility and Site Procurement

Specially designed facilities are needed to serve both older adults and children. First, it is important that the facility be located near bus or subway lines so that older adults who no longer drive have access to the site. It is often wise to locate the site near a school if that particular program plans to work with school-aged children. For example, if it is a child day care, kindergarten or after-school program, children can walk to the center if it is close enough to their school. Within the facility, it is important that there are convenient accesses to upper floors so that older adults will not be unduly inconvenienced. Curbings and walkways need to be designed so that older persons in wheelchairs may go wherever pedestrians go; and ramps and grab bars need to be installed appropriately. At the same time, research and experience has shown that children learn better when they have furniture, toilets, sinks, and play equipment that are scaled down to their size.

Recruitment

Recruitment involves establishing contact with appropriate community agencies that will help identify the participants for the intergenerational program. It is hoped that at this stage collaboration between agencies serving older adults and agencies serving children and youth has been established. If not, it would be wise to schedule presentations to organizations such as schools, youth service organizations, religious and volunteer organizations, civic organizations, senior centers, and residences for older persons. In addition to direct presentations to potential participants, it is desirable to develop a recruitment strategy that includes the use of the media (newspapers, TV, radio) and the use of printed materials (posters, flyers, brochures). The recruitment effort needs to involve several techniques and the cooperation of a variety of groups within the community. Contacts for the recruitment of older adults include the local Area Agency on Aging, senior centers and senior information and referral agencies. Employment Development Departments generally have a worker assigned to assist older applicants. Churches and clubs will often make announcements at their events or in their bulletins.

Large print newspaper ads are effective in both general circulation and specialized newspapers (many communities have newsletters directed to senior groups). Notices can be posted at senior centers, libraries, mobile home communities, churches, and retirement residences. One particularly useful tool is a feature story with photographs in a local newspaper.

Recruitment should begin after the program has received administrative support and commitment from collaborating agencies, and may be accomplished by the project coordinator in conjunction with representatives from the agencies serving older persons, children and youth.

It is important to consider that recruitment usually needs to be ongoing. Attrition and/or expansion require continued recruitment efforts. Once people are recruited, they should be incorporated into the program as soon as possible. Delays commonly cause a loss of participants.

Orientation and Training

Orientation and training refers to those activities designed to enhance the participants' effectiveness in and enjoyment of the intergenerational program. This may include sensitizing youth, elders and staff to age-related issues, helping staff and participants work well together, and preparing the participants for their respective roles. Henkin and Newman report that orientation and training should include a series of formal and informal meetings and/or workshops that help participants:

—understand the goals and objectives of the program
—become confident of their roles and responsibilities in the program
—gain increased awareness of the value of linking the generations
—gain greater insight into their own attitudes about aging
—develop skills necessary to work effectively in an intergenerational program
—understand the systems within which the program is being developed, and
—establish and strengthen positive relationships.

They suggest that after participants have been identified, a sequence of orientation and training experiences should be prepared and scheduled. These should be held during the work day, whenever possible. Commonly, these experiences occur both before the participants begin their involvement in the intergenerational interactions (pre-service) and at intervals throughout the program (in-service). The pre-service experiences provide the participants with the knowledge and skills necessary to get started; the in-service experiences help the participants to improve their skills and learn new skills that will enhance their enjoyment of the intergenerational program (Henkin & Newman, 1985).

Maintenance and Support

Maintenance and support refers to those program activities that are designed to enhance the effectiveness of the program, to provide reinforcement to the participants, and to secure the future of the program. Training, the topic previously discussed, contributes to the maintenance of a strong intergenerational program. Other maintenance and support activities include:

a. *Staff meetings* that reinforce administrative support, provide an opportunity to review short and long range program plans, allow for discussion of evaluation strategies and provide opportunities to design procedures for reinforcing the roles of the participants.
b. *Program development* meetings that provide time to discuss expansion ideas for the program, allow for opportunities to plan special activities that expand or enrich the program, allow time for review of evaluation data to refine and strengthen current program activities and procedures, and offer an opportunity to recommend ideas for new intergenerational programs.
c. *Participant recognition activities* that include formal scheduled recognition events in which the collaborating systems recognize the contributions of the participants (e.g., awards ceremonies, issuance of certificates of service, and official proclamations of thanks); and informal, ongoing acknowledgment of the contributions of the participants in the program (e.g., recognizing participants' birthdays and sharing holiday celebrations).
d. *Special events* that are scheduled to promote participant and community interest, such as intergenerational hobby days, intergenerational community fairs or all age sports days (to name only a few).

These events and activities should occur periodically throughout the program, frequently enough to maintain interest and commitment but not so often as to become burdensome. The actual frequency will vary with the specific activity. Informal recognition, for example, should occur on a daily basis while formal recognition events are usually scheduled as an annual affair. Maintenance and support activities should vary each year to sustain participant interest, and these should respond to the needs and interests of the participants. They can also be used to stimulate community awareness of and interest in the program.

ASSURING LONGEVITY

Probably the most important factor in assuring longevity of a program is strong leadership. Not only should those in a leadership position within the program have professional education and training; they should also have certain attitudes and personality traits which characterize a successful leader of older people.

> Before accepting responsibility to be a leader, an individual needs to evaluate himself and his motives for becoming involved. Is he really interested in utilizing himself and his skills in working with older adults? Does he honestly believe that older adults have equal claim with children and youth for the community's concern and support? . . . "One must have a sincere liking for older people and believe in their potentials to develop new skills, learn new knowledge, and expand their mental and spiritual horizons. The friendly, warm person with a positive outlook on life transmits these attitudes to those with whom he works and enables the program to become a setting in which truly creative encounters can take place between leaders and members and among themselves." (Vickery, 1972)

A strong leader performs management functions and correlates the overall program. The leader shares in program development, works with board and participant councils and/or committees and supervises the work of professional staff. A leader prepares the budget and controls income and expenditures. While performing these administrative and community related tasks, the program leader must also find time to develop a warm one-to-one relationship not only with the staff, board members, and volunteers, but also with as many older and younger participants as possible, developing a sense of community with all of the people involved in the program. The participants and volunteers will look to the program leader for recognition and approval. A leader is to be able to carry out the role assumed in a non-authoritarian approach. Professional education and experience in social work, counseling or psychology, religious education, rehabilitation, recreation, or education are helpful backgrounds from which to develop the administrative skills needed to be an effective leader of an intergenerational program. A leader must have a skill in working with people — the ability to relate meaningfully and yet remain objective in relationships with all individuals in the program.

Interested, skilled and trained professional staff is the next most important factor in determining the effectiveness of intergenerational programs. Without a competent staff, a program will fall apart or stagnate in a monotonous, uninteresting routine. Knowledge of the social and emotional needs of older adults and youth/children in the program is needed in order to work successfully with them. Staff must be able to accept each individual at his level of socialization offering opportunities to enlarge and enrich each person's interest in greater self-fulfillment. As a general rule, the staffing of an intergenerational program will include an executive director, program director, program aides and students in training, teachers, group leaders, counselors, program consultants and perhaps recreation leaders, skill specialists and researchers, depending on the type of intergenerational program. Secretarial, clerical, bookkeeping and maintenance staff are essential. Oftentimes the program will also have volunteers. Some or all of these professionals and paraprofessionals can be older people.

Another aspect to insure longevity in an intergenerational program is public relations. In a *Gerontologist* article, Silverstein states that around every individual exists a formal and informal information network (Silverstein, 1984). An important finding in her study was that respondents did not utilize one source of knowledge for all services. "Rather, respondents learned of some services primarily through informal sources; some through the media; and still others, albeit far fewer, through formal sources." The formal networks are usually the best informed, but older people usually listen to their informal network (those they are involved with during their daily life) first and foremost. She suggests that for programs to be really successful in reaching older participants, the informal networks need to be targeted as much as formal ones. This places a large responsibility upon a program's public relations effort, but it is very necessary for the community to know about and be familiar with the program. As mentioned earlier, making presentations to service agencies and posting flyers and brochures is fine, but it is also important to reach the informal networks of individuals who may be in touch with older adults, and youth/children. Cantor and Mayer (1975) suggest that the pastor is a most important entry point to the informal networks of older adults. This has been true of the Elvirita Lewis Foundation's experience. We found that churches, service clubs and ethnic organizations were very useful and supportive contacts for our intergenerational programs.

NATIONAL FOCUS

Finally, and perhaps most importantly, one should consider bringing a national focus to the issue of intergenerational programming. Change cannot occur unless information reaches decision makers at the local, state and national level, and is subsequently communicated to and accepted by the general public. How can we get intergenerational information to the decision makers? First, we can start with our local, state and federal elected officials: the U. S. House and Senate Aging Committees and large aging organizations who have been successful national advocates for the aging. Intergenerational programs also work for youth; therefore, it is necessary to contact the cadre of organizations, agencies and committees committed to youth and children. Approaching programming in this way permits advocacy for intergenerational programs to continue to grow and the wheel is not continually being reinvented. Program successes can be catalogued, followed and incorporated into appropriate networks such as the affiliated associations of the National Council on Aging, special intergenerational organizations like Generations United, the National Coalition for Intergenerational Resources, the National Association of Foster Grandparent Directors and the National Association for the Education of Young People.

According to Kerschner and Hirschfield (Kerschner, 1975), a

vast percentage of public policy has been derived from the onset of a crisis.

> The Social Security Act, for example, did not grow out of a long-planned move to insert the federal government into the economy on a massive scale. Rather, the Social Security Act was a direct outgrowth of the crisis of the Depression. Once the initial shock hit and people began to lose their jobs, it became apparent that older workers were being deprived of occupations, incomes, and savings.

The demographic tidal wave of aged that will hit us in the early 2000s could create another economic crisis. We are hardly prepared for the onslaught of millions of unemployed, underused and undervalued older persons whose economic needs we must address. Coupled with this projected economic condition of older persons there will be an unprecedented number of women entering the workforce and leaving our children/youth largely inadequately cared for. Must it once again require a crisis of not being able to care for our elderly and children to spur legislation for intergenerational programming? Let us hope not. Rather, let us do everything in our power to inform the powers-that-be about the importance of intergenerational programming before we see the crisis at hand.

REFERENCES

Cantor, M. & Mayer, M. (1975). *Factors in differential utilization of service by urban elderly*. Paper presented at the 28th Annual Scientific Meeting of the Gerontological Society of America, Louisville, KY.

Classon, G. (1982). *The Richest Man in Babylon*. New York: Bantam Books.

Henkin, N. & Newman, S. (1985). *An instuctional guide to "The best of you . . . The best of me."* Harrisburg, PA: Department of Aging.

Johnson, S. & Siegel, W. (1980). *Bridging Generations: A handbook for intergenerational child care*. Palm Springs: The Elvirita Lewis Foundation, The Elder Press.

Kent, D., Kastenbaum, R., & Sherwood, S. (Eds.). (1979). *Research planning and action for the elderly: The power and potential of social science*, New York: Human Sciences Press.

Kerschner, P. (Ed.) (1979). *Advocacy and Age: Issues, experiences, strategies*. Los Angeles, CA: University of Southern California, Andrus Gerontology Center.

Kerschner, P. & Herschfield, I. (1975). *Public policy and aging*. In J. Berren & D. Woodruff (Eds.), *Aging: Scientific perspectives and social issues*. (pp. 356-357). New York: Van Nostrand.

Naisbitt, J. (1982). *Megatrends: Ten new directions transforming our lives*, New York: Warner Books.

Silverstein, N. (1984, February). Informing the elderly about public services: The relationship between sources of knowledge and service utilization. *The Gerontologist, 24*(1), 37-40.

Tice, C., & Warren, B. (1988). *Developing and evaluating intergenerational programs*. Unpublished manuscript.

Vickery, F. (1972). *Creative programming for older adults: A leadership training guide*. New York: Association Press.

Training and Education
for Intergenerational Activities:
An Agenda for the Future

Karen Vander Ven, PhD

SUMMARY. This paper presents a variety of issues that intersect in preparing personnel for intergenerational work. It addresses such issues as the scope of intergenerational practice, the expanded roles of personnel in intergenerational programs, the various competencies and skills needed for work, and the need to integrate intergenerational preparation into the formal systems of training and education for human services. The author suggests that the final challenge in the advancement and training of practitioners for intergenerational work is the establishment of academic sponsorship in the field of intergenerational practice.

Our children are progressing so well. I'm sure it's due at least in part to the activities of our older volunteers. Their training program really is helping them to contribute positively.

I'm going to feel a lot more comfortable directing a social service agency with a course in intergenerational program development and administration in my study plan.

I never thought I'd go for a post-retirement career change, and look at me now—I'm a Child Development Associate and working in a day care center!

Karen Vander Ven is Professor in the Program in Child Development and Child Care, School of Social Work, University of Pittsburgh, 1717 Cathedral of Learning, Pittsburgh, PA 15260.

BACKGROUND

These quotes reflect various situations in human service delivery that can be positively addressed by appropriate activities that prepare personnel specifically in intergenerational work.

Fortunately, such preparation has begun and with some promising initial results. It is important that this beginning be extended by further identifying more precisely the scope of intergenerational work, the competencies needed to perform it, and the formalization and standardization of training and education needed for practice. Issues around preparing those persons who work in them must be addressed so intergenerational work can continue to actualize its potential rather than fall prey to the disillusionment that has occurred historically when promising social interventions have been mounted without sufficient attention to practitioners' knowledge and skill.

The Significance of Preparation for Intergenerational Practice

It is now acknowledged that specific preparation for the job to be done is related to the success of human service endeavors. This has been underscored for the general field of aging by Klegon (1980) who presents evidence to support training and professionalism among its practitioners. The case has been even more compellingly clear in the field of child care with such findings as those of Ruopp (1979) who states that there is a positive relationship between the child development preparation of practitioners and the positive outcomes for children. A properly prepared staff is an essential component of a high quality child care program. Similarly, the intent of preparation for intergenerational work should be to develop professionalism in the staff that enables them to create a quality program for both elders and younger persons.

Current knowledge indicates that intergenerational programs have already shown that they yield positive outcomes such as increased self-esteem, sense of personal value, learning ability, general well-being, and understanding of others, for both the younger and older participants. However, at this point it is not yet known to what degree which skills are directly related to such outcomes, and whether there are many other potential skills that have not yet been identified.

It is reasonable to suggest, therefore, that intergenerational programs are more likely to achieve positive outcomes if those who conduct them are prepared in related knowledge and skills. In order to do this, training and education issues must be addressed in order to continue to advance effective intergenerational practice. This paper will present such an agenda.

AN AGENDA OF ISSUES IN PREPARING PERSONNEL FOR INTERGENERATIONAL WORK

Recognition of the Scope of Intergenerational Practice

Intergenerational work needs to be recognized in all its complexity if personnel preparation activities are to be adequate. The core definition of intergenerational programming is

> Planned activities and experiences that are designed to bring generations together for their mutual benefit. These activities and experiences must be ongoing and systematic, must continue for an extended period of time at regular intervals and must benefit all participants — youth, older persons, and staff. (Henkin & Newman, 1985)

It is important to recognize that an intergenerational program is not a unitary or invariant construct. Some think that intergenerational programming only means older adults being the initiators of activities with children in sites that primarily serve children. It should be emphasized that some programs conversely involve children and youth who may require orientation and preparation in programs and agencies serving the elderly. There is a great variety of specific combinations of youth and older adults that can be made to form a particular intergenerational program.

There are generic preparation activities that will allow personnel, whether old or young, to apply basic knowledge and skills across various sub-groups, settings and program models as long as they can also make adaptations to individual situations. The development of such generic preparation is one of the major tasks for the advancement of intergenerational programs in the future.

There are a variety of intergenerational roles for both older and younger participants for which training and education activities must be differentiated. These roles include direct interaction in core and enrichment functions, and the consideration of children and youth as concurrent providers as well as receivers of intergenerational services.

Direct Work. Personnel preparation in human services has traditionally begun by targeting those who work directly with clients. This has also been true of intergenerational work. In intergenerational training, the training activities that exist such as orientation activities, in-service training, supervisory programs have been heretofore primarily targeted toward the older adults, but if the nature of intergenerational programs is reciprocal, then direct training for children and youth is also necessary. As a general premise, it seems appropriate that the older the youth, the more likely some kind of formal training might be a prerequisite.

Core and Enrichment Roles. Training must consider whether older adults provide enrichment to a program or if they are core staff. The difference is that a core staff assumes primary responsibilities essential for a program to operate while enrichment staff enhances a program by providing additional stimulation, resources, activities and relationship opportunities.

In general, those on the enrichment staff function as volunteers while those on the core staff are salaried. Most training to date in intergenerational programming has been for volunteer roles which require less formal education requirements.

However, there is a growing trend towards considering older adults as primary staff as well as volunteers in child care programs (*New York Times*, 1987). The rationale for this is that the increase in numbers of working mothers will be accompanied by a much greater need for child care workers, a need that might not be sufficiently filled by younger people. This suggests that preparation of older persons as primary child care workers needs to be increasingly related to standard and recognized preparation models for child care workers of any age. This should be done to assure that children served receive optimum quality care, and also that older adults who assume the responsibilities of skilled child care work will not be exploited by being inadequately compensated or undervalued.

Indirect Practice. There has been increasing recognition in human service fields that personnel need to be prepared not only for direct service roles, but also for "indirect" ones as well. These include such functions as program planning, development and coordination, staff supervision, training, assessment, program monitoring, evaluation, and work with other systems. The need for training in these areas was the rationale for the "Cascade Model" for intergenerational child care programs in which task- and objectives-based training activities were specifically designed for program administrators, coordinators, supervisors and child care providers of intergenerational programs (Newman, Ehrlich, & Vander Ven, 1988). When training targets all levels of personnel, the probability of program success as an integrated system is greatly increased.

Systematic Identification of Competencies and Skills for Intergenerational Work

The training that has accompanied intergenerational programs has been delivered in the form of agency sponsored workshops and seminars or as individual technical assistance from organized intergenerational programs that provide training to others. The content of this training has generally been based upon the previous experience of the trainers and utilization of published program descriptions, monographs, and other resource materials from such organizations as the Beverly Foundation, Generations Together, and the Elvirita Lewis Foundation (Ehrlich, Newman, & Vander Ven, 1987; Seefeldt, 1985; Struntz & Reville, 1985; Thorp, 1985; Tice, 1985).

As invaluable as these resources are, both as evidence of the phenomenal growth of intergenerational activities and as sources for training activities, there is still an inconsistency and fragmentation in training. What is offered in one agency may be completely different from that offered in another, and may be so specific that the content is not transferable to another setting or program, thereby diminishing its value.

To enhance its utility and legitimacy, intergenerational programming now needs to move into developing competency- or objectives-based training, the various roles involved in intergenerational work that are designed to meet the needs of the clients and settings in a wide variety of intergenerational activities.

Toward this end, a major task analysis (observing and analyzing what people are actually doing in conducting intergenerational activities) should be mounted. Task analysis is a well-known method for deriving training objectives and designing supportive curriculum (Mager & Beach, 1967; Mager & Pipe, 1970). A national initiative should be organized to do this, perhaps utilizing the successful competency-based child development associate (DCA) model, or the DACUM curriculum development model (1977) both of which have been useful in identifying competency clusters for child care workers.

The ultimate mission of this activity would be to identify basic competencies associated with standard roles and levels of practice, to organize them into meaningful modules, and to develop mechanisms for their dissemination and formal adoption.

INTEGRATION OF INTERGENERATIONAL PREPARATION INTO THE FORMAL SYSTEM OF TRAINING AND EDUCATION FOR HUMAN SERVICES WORK

Once basic competencies have been identified and organized, then the task is to integrate the results into the formal system for preparing practitioners for human service work. Here the distinction between training and education is reiterated.

Training refers to specific information and skill development which is provided in order to enable persons to do a specific job in a specific setting. It is primarily concerned with "how to" in the immediate situation, rather than with "why." Education, on the other hand, is concerned with broader perspectives: providing a conceptual base for the framing of information; inculcating thinking and problem solving skills that permit the practitioner to be able to adapt practice to emerging and future needs; and encouraging long-term transferability of knowledge and skill (Vander Ven, 1985).

In order for intergenerational practice to achieve its optimal effectiveness, *both* training and education need to be available, and it needs to be organized in a way that is congruent with established levels of preparation and recognized career ladders.

Training: Pre- and In-Service

Systematizing the training activity for intergenerational work involves framing it in the standard pre-service, in-service training model. Pre-service training provides new practitioners sufficient skill and information to perform at the entry level. An example would be the orientation given to older volunteers who are recruited into an intergenerational program. In-service training is intended to build upon previous knowledge and to develop new knowledge, the content of which may be contained within various disciplines (e.g., nursing, social work, and early childhood development). Generations Together, at the University of Pittsburgh, for example, has offered an interdisciplinary course, "Intergenerational Experiences in Society" under sponsorship of the School of Social Work.

Education

The formalization of educational activities is important because it is graduates of the current human service disciplines who will, or should be, aware of the great power of intergenerational activities as a developmental and therapeutic intervention.

A major issue affecting integration of intergenerational activities into the educational system is that the sponsorship or home base of the field of intergenerational practice has not yet been formally established. Because intergenerational programs serve two populations (children and older adults) with dissimilar preparation of personnel from two discrete disciplines that structurally are not connected, "child care education," and "geriatric and gerontological education" makes this task challenging, but not insurmountable. The very nature of intergenerational work makes it an ideal field to encourage the interdisciplinary collaborations that many universities today are hoping to promote. This factor might fuel attempts to more systematically incorporate intergenerational training into these settings.

Intergenerational objectives appropriate to the specific discipline should be incorporated into academic courses on gerontology, and the child development and child care courses for human service practitioners such as nurses, and social workers. These would include courses and sequences in degree programs and continuing education activities. It is important that clinical practice or field work in intergenerational settings be included in *educational* preparation for human service work.

The growing trend to look upon older adults as paraprofessional and paid providers of child care suggests that formal preparation of personnel will increasingly occur, and it will be sponsored within the credential awarding capacity of institutions of higher education, possibly in conjunction with organized state or federal training programs such as the Child Development Associate and the Job Partnership Training Act (Jackson & Colberly, 1985). Those involved in the initiative to professionalize child care will stress the need for all practitioners with children, no matter what their age, to be properly prepared. This will serve as a further impetus to establish intergenerational education within college and university settings.

IDENTIFICATION OF INSTRUCTIONAL METHODS FOR ADULT LEARNERS OF INTERGENERATIONAL WORK

Although all effective efforts in training and education are predicated upon recognition of learner attributes and associated adaptations of instructional design and teaching strategies, it is particularly important that these be considered in intergenerational training and education. This is highly relevant for older adults whose competency can be greatly enhanced when instructional strategies are designed that build upon their wealth of previous experience and recognize both their physical and cognitive capacities.

A systematic review of learning styles of older adults, and designs of adult education should be incorporated into the content and structure of intergenerational training. It can be anticipated that instructional activities such as role playing, simulation, games (Bonstelle & Govoni, 1984) group problem solving, peer sharing and coaching, audiovisuals and similar experiential methods will be among those found to be suitable.

Sensitivity to learning styles of potential intergenerational practitioners can be achieved without compromising the development of competencies and standards for practice. Adapting instruction to learner characteristics simply makes it more likely that they will be able to perform the tasks for which they are being prepared.

RESEARCH PROGRAMS FOCUSING ON INTERGENERATIONAL THEORY AND PRACTICE

As preparation for intergenerational work continues, it will be important to move towards identifying those variables in programs and practitioner competencies that are directly related to positive results for all participants. This will require systematic research in such variables as identified interventions-identified outcomes, pre- and post-program evaluation, effects of various pairings; and specific practitioner competencies and impact on clients (see Bocian & Newman in this edition). As results are yielded, they can be related back to the training and education system by deriving instructional objectives and curricular components that specifically prepare practitioners to be able to deliver the interventions that are established as being effective.

This research activity should also contribute to the most important function of *theory building*. To advance intergenerational work, there must be a core theory dealing with its sources of knowledge, its fundamental premises, its functions, its recipients, and its outcomes, which as it grows can generate new research questions and infuse the education and practice system with continued vitality and growth.

ACADEMIC SPONSORSHIP OF INTERGENERATIONAL WORK

A final challenge facing the advancement of training and education of practitioners is the establishment of academic sponsorship of the field of intergenerational practice. The function of this sponsorship would be to encourage expansion of the knowledge base of intergenerational work, and to promote program development, education, and research. Since intergenerational work embraces two client populations that are already provided standard services of established human service professions, it does not seem to specifically fit into any one of them more than another. This has two implications: one, is that it could be "housed" compatibly in any of several professions that prepares human service personnel in a particular profession (e.g., social work, nursing, education). The other is that it might be an integral part of a completely new sponsoring field and hence belong there. This new field may then be identified as "developmental life cycle caregiving" which would deal specifically with developmental interventions for individuals throughout the life cycle (Vander Ven, 1986). The rationale for this proposed new profession is based on similarities between child care and youth care work and care of older adults, and on the fact that there are common developmental and caregiving needs of persons from birth to old age that could be served by one field of generically prepared practitioners. This field, should it actually emerge, might eventually be the fundamental and logical home base of intergenerational studies.

In the meantime, consideration of all of the previously cited issues in training education might contribute toward empowering intergenerational practice to achieve its goals.

REFERENCES

Bonstelle, S. & Govoni, A. (1984, March-April). Into aging: Exploring aging through games. *Rehabilitation Nursing*, pp. 24-27.

Elvirita Lewis Foundation. (1980). *Current programs using elders in child care*. Soquel, CA: Author.

Ehrlich, L., Vander Ven, K., Newman, S. & McIntyre, K. (1986). *Children and older adults learn and live together: A training model for planning and conducting intergenerational programs in child care centers*. Unpublished manuscript, University of Pittsburgh, Generations Together.

Ehrlich, L., Newman, S. & Vander Ven, K. (1987). *Training for successful implementation of intergenerational programs in child care settings: The Cascade Model*. Unpublished manuscript, University of Pittsburgh, Generations Together.

The extension of the child development associate credentialing system. (1981, June). New York: Bank Street College of Education.

Henkin, N. & Newman, S. (1985). *An instructional guide to "The Best of You . . . The Best of Me."* Harrisburg: The Pennsylvania Department of Aging.

Jackson, M. & Coberly, S. (1985). *Older workers and the job training partnership act: A survey and case study analysis of three percent set-aside programs*.

Los Angeles, CA: University of Southern California, Andrus Gerontology Center, National Policy Center on Employment and Retirement.

Katz, L. (1984, July). The professional early childhood teacher. *Young Children*, *39*(5), pp. 3-10.

Klegon, D. (1980). Education and attitudes toward training and professionalism among practitioners in the field of aging. *Educational Gerontologist*, *5*, 211-224.

Klein, J. & Lombardi, J. (1982, November-December). Training early childhood teachers: The CDA Program. *Children Today*, *11*(6), pp. 2-6.

Mager, R. & Beach, K. (1967). *Developing vocational instruction*. Belmont, CA: Fearon Publishers.

Mager, R. & Pipe, P. (1970). *Analyzing performance problems or "you really ought wanna."* Belmont, CA: Fearon Publishers.

Provincial program guidelines for child care worker in Ontario colleges of applied arts and technology. (1977). Ontario: Ontario Social Services.

Seefeldt, C., Jantz, R., Serock, K. & Bredekamp, S. (1979). *Young and old together: A training manual for intergenerational programs*. College Park: University of Maryland, College of Education, Center on Aging. (ERIC Document Reproduction Service No. ED 210 089)

Struntz, K. & Reville, S. (1985). *Growing together: An intergenerational sourcebook*. Washington, DC: American Association of Retired Persons, Palm Springs, CA: The Elvirita Lewis Foundation.

Ruopp, R., Travers, J., Glantz, S. & Coelen, C. (1979). Children at the center: Summary findings and their implications. In final report of the *National Day Care Study Vol. 1*. Cambridge, MA: Abt Associates.

A time and a place for sharing: A practical guide for developing programs. (1984). Pasadena, CA: The Beverly Foundation.

Thorp, K. (Ed.). (1985). *Intergenerational programs: A resource for community renewal*. Madison: Wisconsin Positive Youth Development Initiative.

Tice, C. (1985, September/October). Perspectives on intergenerational initiatives past, present and future. *Children Today*, *14*(5), 6-11.

U.S. Department of Health and Human Services. (1987). *Directory of curriculum guidelines for geriatric education*. Washington, DC: Public Health Service, Health Resources and Services Administration, Bureau of Health Professions.

Vander Ven, K. (1986, Spring). From child care to developmental life cycle caregiving: A proposal for future growth. *Journal of Child and Youth Care Work*, *2*, 53-62.

Vander Ven, K. (1986, March). *The intergenerational perspective as an initiator and integrator of life span theory and practice*. Paper presented at the meeting of the Association for Gerontology in Higher Education, Atlanta, GA.

Vander Ven, K. (1985). "You've come a long way baby: The evolution and significance of caregiving" and "And you have a way to go: The current status and emerging issues in training and education for child care practice." In K. Vander Ven & E. Tittnich (Eds.), *Competent Caregivers: Competent Children*. New York: Haworth Press.

Evaluation of Intergenerational Programs: Why and How?

Kathleen Bocian, MEd
Sally Newman, PhD

SUMMARY. This paper presents a rationale for evaluating intergenerational programs and describes some of the unique considerations and basic components inherent in these evaluations. It systematically describes strategies and methodologies associated with this process and concludes with a statement of some insights that can result from careful and serious evaluation efforts.

The papers in this edition have articulated the need for and benefits of intergenerational programs in our society. There is an assumption inherent in each paper that intergenerational programming is a good thing, and that they have multiple impacts on the participants, the agency staff and the surrounding community. As we move to promote intergenerational concepts in the next decade more than assumptions are needed. Solid data are needed from intergenerational programs that have been developed, field tested, revised and evaluated.

Evaluation of intergenerational programs is necessary for a variety of reasons. These reasons include:

- *To assess the program.* Were the program goals and objectives realized? What is the impact of the program on the participants?
- *To define areas of needed program change.* To what degree

Kathleen Bocian is Development Officer and Sally Newman is Executive Director for Generations Together, 811 William Pitt Union, University of Pittsburgh, Pittsburgh, PA 15260.

are staff and/or participant expectations being met? What gaps exist between goals and outcomes? How effective were the program implementation procedures?

- *To increase public knowledge about the program.* What does the program look like: the demographics of the participants, the type of activities, the roles and responsibilities of the individual participants and systems?
- *To garner community support for the program.* How do program goals meet the assessed needs in the community? What underserved population is addressed through the programming efforts?
- *To determine the appropriateness of the program for replication.* What are the essential components for program success? What are the anticipated differences of program operation with different locales and populations?
- *To secure funding for expansion and/or maintenance of program.* What problems in the community are addressed by the program? What measurable decrease in these problems can be attributed to the presence of an intergenerational program?

In addition to reflecting these short-term program outcomes, comprehensive evaluation of intergenerational programs can become a barometer of long-term change. Evaluation can underscore the need for ongoing collaboration between systems and can affect the future development of agencies through integration of intergenerational programs. Further, evaluation efforts can address some of the unique social issues that are a function of the demographic changes in our society: family mobility, substantial years of healthy living after retirement and a population bulge of frail elders dependent on a decreasing labor force.

UNIQUE FEATURES OF INTERGENERATIONAL PROGRAM EVALUATION

In addition to these issues, intergenerational programs present some unique features to be considered that may not be evident in other social service program evaluation efforts. These features include:

1. Two very different client populations participating in the program, necessitating different methods of collecting evaluative data.
2. Two discrete and independent agencies or systems implementing the intergenerational program and involved in the evaluation effort.
3. Diverse program outcome data that include affective and cognitive impact on the program participants and performance impact on the staff.
4. The opportunity to address social issues through a process of interagency collaboration and cross-generational exchange.

The parameters and special evaluation considerations for each of these four features is described in the following sections.

Differing Client Populations

The persons served by intergenerational programs are drawn from a population with diverse economic, racial and ethnic backgrounds. They represent mainstream, special needs or at-risk children and youth of preschool through college age. They include youth in typical educational settings such as child care centers or schools, and atypical settings such as foster homes, or facilities that house physically, psychologically or emotionally impaired youth. Participants in intergenerational programs also represent the elderly population over 55 who are well or frail, who are living independently or in supportive settings such as nursing homes or personal care facilities. These older persons reflect diverse life skills, work experiences and cultural backgrounds.

Each of these groups, by their very nature, present different variables that should be assessed in evaluation efforts. The selection of these variables is further influenced by the characteristics of the specific participants and by the specific nature of the intergenerational interaction. For example, it is reasonable to consider maintenance of cognitive functioning in frail Alzheimer's patients if the intergenerational program is focused on frequent, therapeutic stimulation provided by trained college students; this is not a reasonable point of assessment if the intergenerational program is built around bi-weekly social activities between Alzheimer's patients in a day care facility and a local Girl Scout troop.

Discrete Systems or Agencies

The complexities of two different systems within an evaluation effort are partly based on the different values each agency may hold related to evaluation procedures, data and dissemination. Each agency has different staffing patterns, different protocols and different training procedures. Program implementation (even of the same program) varies among agencies as does the need for training in execution of the evaluation.

Agencies collaborating on intergenerational program evaluation need to establish common evaluation goals and priorities. Once established, specialized training in the data collection may be appropriate for the collaborating program staff. Further support must be available to sustain evaluation efforts. This support takes the form of establishing evaluation as a priority within agency efforts, providing the time and resources necessary to complete evaluation efforts, considering evaluative data and analysis as helpful indicators for change and using evaluative data when structuring future programs.

Diverse Program Outcome Data

Evaluations of intergenerational programs reflect multiple program outcomes: affective and cognitive outcomes for the program participants, and performance outcomes for the staff.

Within each program is the potential for evaluating its affective outcomes by reporting participant change in areas such as self-esteem, life satisfaction, motivation, and attitude. Similarly, data can be accessed that report participant change in cognitive areas such as learning, memory and activities of daily living. Program impact on the staff performance can be demonstrated through their skill development, level of collaboration, creativity, motivation and commitment to the program.

Within each of these domains, there is an opportunity to use different methods of data collection. A variety of methods provide a more comprehensive evaluation, assuring coverage of variables that might have been overlooked, or that might have appeared insignificant with other certain testing procedures. One example of this from the work of Newman, Vasudev and Onawola (1985) is the assessment of life satisfaction among seniors in school volunteer programs. While there were no significant differences among experienced or new volunteers in life satisfaction as measured by a standardized scale (LIZD, Neugarten, Havighurst & Tobin, 1961), the interview data presented valuable information about the impact of the volunteer experience on the life satisfaction of older adults. These data are important in evaluating the program's worth, and in designing future intergenerational program impact.

Addressing Social Issues

Within our urban and suburban communities are growing social issues which affect our youth and our elderly. Intergenerational programming, which depends on systematic collaboration among those agencies serving younger and older populations, can begin to address some of these issues such as the reduction of services to frail elders, the increase in substance abuse by both younger and older persons and the rise in teen pregnancies and school dropouts. Often the intergenerational programs that tackle these problems promote responsible citizenship within a community (see Moody & Disch, this edition) due to the heightened awareness and increased problem ownership among the intergenerational volunteers. The social impact of cross generational exchange necessitates a different level of evaluation. Longitudinal studies of benefits to participants (pre- and post-program awareness surveys, attitudinal studies among a cross-section of the community's population, experimental and control group studies of the incidence of certain problems, and cost-effectiveness studies for the provision of services to clients) are all appropriate evaluation strategies to be considered in assessing aspects of social impact. Although this level of evaluation and the accompanying methodology appears formidable, it is this type of evaluation that can save intergenerational programs during periods of scarce resources and budget cuts (see Saltz, this edition).

STRATEGIES, COMPONENTS
AND METHODOLOGIES

Evaluation of intergenerational programs may focus on the problem areas of program development, the benefits of intergenerational interaction for participants, or the role of systems in creating and maintaining these intergenerational programs. More comprehensive evaluation efforts may address a combination of these concerns or may examine the societal issues raised in intergenerational programming. Regardless of the evaluation focus, decisions must be made about the strategies, components and methodology of intergenerational program evaluation prior to program startup.

Decisions related to evaluation strategies involve preparing staff and participants for a process that encompasses three specific points:

1. Evaluation that is integral to the program.
2. Evaluation that occurs at both the formative and summative stages of program implementation.
3. Evaluation that is utilization focused.

Each of these strategies is explained in greater detail in the following sections.

Integral Evaluation

In its simplest form, program evaluation can be broken down into four basic steps: planning for the data to be collected, collecting the data, analyzing the data, and presenting the analysis to appropriate audiences. These components do not exist independently of each other, and staff that are to implement the program should be involved in program evaluation decisions at the very beginning. Beyond input in the decision making process of evaluation, the program budget for staff time and dollars should include appropriate emphasis on evaluation with consideration included for outside evaluators, if necessary. The data collected should not be ignored until the close of the program, but should be examined at designated mileposts during the program implementation. Both the process and the quality of the collected data can be assessed through the following questions:

—Are the questions and instruments appropriate for the participants?
—Are the data being collected in a timely fashion, or is there a lag in the collection process?
—Are the data appropriate for assessment of the program objectives?
—Are the data indicative of a particular program implementation problem that should be examined now?
—Are the data diversified enough to address all aspects of the program?

Formative and Summative Phases of Evaluation Procedures

Formative evaluation functions as a barometer of program success. It provides for periodic assessment of program development, and its key function is to enable program revision to occur in a timely fashion during a program's development. Because this evaluation process is ongoing, it usually focuses on the implementation procedures.

Typical formative evaluation questions related to implementation may examine what recruitment method was most successful with volunteers and why, what orientation and training components were most helpful in the actual program activities, and what program activities engendered the desired responses from participants. Such responses may include increased independence in activities of daily living for elders, increased time on task with school work for children, and positive perceptions of elderly and youth from their younger or older counterparts.

Summative evaluation focuses on the outcomes and the conclusion of the program. It is a comprehensive review of all aspects of the program upon its conclusion. It reports on the program's results, the outcomes of each component of the program's implementation and on the impact of the program in relationship to the program's goals and objectives. Ideally, the direct program outcomes are correlated with the intent of the program (see Vander Ven, this edition). Because summative evaluation focuses on outcomes, data from this phase of the evaluation process may be reviewed by persons outside the intergenerational programming effort and may form the basis of future program recommendations.

Some examples of typical outcome evaluation data are presented in Table 1 *Attitudes of Elders Working with Children in Schools*, which represents 3 years of cumulative data collected from the Generations Together Senior Citizen School Volunteer Program in Pittsburgh, Pennsylvania. These elders are involved in the school setting for an average of 4 hours weekly during the school year.

The change reflected here is based on the elders' self-report at the close of the school year. The areas selected for evaluation are related to quality of life for the elders and the elders' perception of the school and community in general. Equally important are data relevant to the youth participating in this intergenerational program. Table 2 *Attitudes of Students Working with Elders* also represents 3 years of cumulative data about young participants in the Senior Citi-

Table 1

Attitudes of Elders Working with Children in Schools
Senior Citizen School Volunteer Program
Cumulative Data 1983-1986

Question Category	Percentage of Total Respondents			
How has your volunteer experience changed your.....	A great deal	Somewhat	Not sure	Not at all
Feeling of being needed	73.2%	13.6%	11.8%	1.3%
Openness to new ideas	54.3%	16.3%	26.8%	2.4%
Self-esteem	53.8%	18.6%	23.1%	1.6%
Attitude toward children and youth	38.6%	30.7%	23.4%	0
Attitude toward public schools	37.5%	32.5%	22.6%	7.4%
Involvement in community activities	37.3%	21.8%	32.8%	8.4%
Knowledge and skills	35.7%	25.7%	35.4%	3.1%

Table 2
Attitudes of Students Working with Elders
Senior Citizen School Volunteer Program
Cumulative Data 1983-1986

Category of Question	Percentage of Total Respondents (n=515)		
How has the presence of an older volunteer affected your students':	Positively	Not sure	Not at all
Self-esteem	86.0%	8.0%	1.4%
Academic growth	83.4%	13.7%	3.0%
Social growth	78.8%	11.3%	15.9%
Attitudes towards older persons	70.3%	24.9%	0.6%
Life skills	60.2%	23.5%	10.7%

zen School Volunteer Program. These data were reported by the teachers of the students participating in the program.

Students involved in this model were in grades 1-12 (with the largest number in grades 1-6) in 10 school districts in western Pennsylvania.

Outcome data of this kind can be collected for all variations of intergenerational programs. As mentioned previously, the questions asked and the type of younger and older participants, volunteers and staff will determine the strategies for data collection and evaluation.

Utilization Focused Evaluation

The specific outcome measures illustrated in Tables 1 and 2 were selected because they were important to the program developer in the Senior Citizen School Volunteer Program. They reflect the values of the developer as stated in the purpose of the program: to effect positive attitudes across generations, and to provide academic assistance to students. If the evaluative data focused on solely the elders' or the youths' growth in knowledge and skill, the evaluation would not have contained all relevant information.

The notion that evaluative data should be useful to those involved in program decision making is identified by Patton (1978) as utilization-focused evaluation. Patton's definition of utilization-focused evaluation is as follows: "utilization occurs when there is an immediate, concrete and observable effect on specific decisions and program activities resulting directly from research findings" (p. 24).

When considering evaluative strategies for programs, Patton suggests that the questions asked by evaluators will be most effective if they meet these five criteria:

1. The question is empirically testable.
2. The question can yield more than one possible answer.
3. The question is important to decision makers and staff.
4. The answer is important to decision makers and staff.
5. The data will be useful in policy making or program development.

Evaluation Components

The components of the evaluation process normally separate into three types: demographic, programmatic and impact. All three are important elements of the intergenerational program, as illustrated by the examples below.

Demographic data. Demographic data indicate the type of participants in the intergenerational program. These data should be collected at the inception and during the life of the program and should include the variables of age, sex, level of education, economic status (where appropriate), and ethnic background. The data are valuable in and of themselves; however, when combined with programmatic or impact data, they provide rich information to both policy makers and program planners.

Programmatic data. Programmatic data reflect the procedures of the intergenerational program in practice: the hours, the types of activities, their duration and frequency. These categories are relevant in every aspect of the intergenerational program (e.g., volunteer recruitment and training, staff orientation and training, the actual intergenerational activities and maintenance and support efforts) (see Brummel, this edition). The usefulness of these data depend on the balance achieved between structural aspects of the program (hours, numbers and kind of activity) and the dynamic aspects of the program (the nature of interactions among staff, volunteers and other participants, outreach into the community, and the unspoken goals of administrators and volunteers). The structural aspects of the program may say less than do the dynamic aspects of program quality, which require more subtle and laborious methods of assessment (Gurland, Bennett & Wilder, 1984).

Impact data. Impact data may be directed towards cognitive, physical, attitudinal or societal change resulting from participation in intergenerational programming. These data are particularly useful to potential funders of intergenerational programs and policy makers in general. When impact evaluation data is to be used for this purpose, it needs to be tied to the needs assessment that prompted the intergenerational program, and/or the training inherent in the program (see Vander Ven, this edition).

The credibility of impact evaluation data is strengthened if some comparison group is involved in the measurement of change. This comparison could be of the same participants, prior to and post program implementation, or a comparison of program participants to a "control" group that has not participated in intergenerational programming. The easiest control may be already published "norms" for the variables of interest. The caution in this instance is to establish that the intergenerational program participants are similar in pertinent demographic variables to the group that established the norm. Matched control groups provide the most power to evaluative data. However, care must be exercised when comparing participants across systems. The notion of successful intergenerational programming is dependent on system collaboration, therefore, a competitive evaluation procedure could be counterproductive.

Methodology

Methods for collecting and analyzing evaluative data are dependent on program participants, the available time and expertise of staff, and the kind of information needed.

There are several basic methods of evaluation that can be utilized in assessing intergenerational programs:

— informal observations
— structured observations
— self-report questionnaires
— objective tests and measures
— interviews

Informal Observations. In informal observations the program evaluator reports the feelings of the intergenerational participants in their own terms, as stated in informal meetings and as a result of unstructured and undirected discussions. Another aspect of informal observations includes the evaluators' reports on observed overall personal interaction in the program and on the overall gestalt (general tone) of the environment in which the intergenerational program is being implemented.

Data collected from informal observations can include quotes from participants, anecdotes reporting on observed interaction, and notes on the substance and quality of interactions amongst and between participants and staff. Informal observation is valuable as a wholistic approach to program evaluation, and as a field-based guide to determining future evaluation questions.

Structured Observations. Structured observations are systematic in terms of their selection of subjects, the selection of time and setting, and the content and scoring of the observation itself. Structured observations can be used to demonstrate change in behavior or interactions over a period of time. Examples of structured observation instruments or schedules include the Flanders Interaction Analysis and its Adaptation for Intergenerational Programs (OPSCI) (Newman & Onawola, 1986), Nursing Assessment Observation Log (in Lyons & Newman, 1983).

Self-Report Questionnaire. Self-reporting questionnaires yield data about people's perception of their feelings, attitudes and activities. These questionnaires may involve a combination of open and closed ended questions, and may include items from a variety of sources. These questionnaires are used extensively in attitudinal research, and can be very effective in the program evaluation process. In intergenerational programs, self-report questionnaires are appropriate for persons who are capable of reflecting their own feelings about the program. Other tools are used for participants who find this method of evaluation difficult such as young children or disoriented frail elders.

A variety of self-report instruments exist that are appropriate for evaluation of intergenerational programs. These instruments include:

- Life Satisfaction Index — LIZD (Neugarten, Havighurst & Tobin, 1961)
- Children's Attitudes Toward Elderly — CATE (Seefeldt, Jantz, Galper & Serock, 1977)
- Children's Views on Aging — CVoA (Hanusa, Marks, Newman & Onawola, 1988)
- Semantic Differential Scale (Osgood, Suel & Tannenbaum, 1957)

For intergenerational program evaluation, a self-report questionnaire designed specifically for the program may be helpful. Even a fairly simple questionnaire can yield powerful results if completed by different groups and then examined for common variances. An excellent example of recent intergenerational research that used study-specific instruments is Mangen, Bengtson and Landry, Jr.'s study of three generation population during the 1970s in California (*Measurement of Intergenerational Relations*, 1988).

Objective Tests and Measures. Objective tests and measures may be completed by the complete range of intergenerational program participants. For this type of evaluation, it is best to select an existing instrument, and as much as possible, to select instruments that are already in use by the system hosting the intergenerational program. For example, patient assessment tools used in nursing homes may provide valuable data about increased patient activity and alertness correlating with the onset of intergenerational programming. Student weekly or monthly test scores can show a change in pupils' performance as a result of direct weekly support provided by older persons as classroom volunteers. The implementation and accuracy of the evaluation will be much simpler and stronger if the staff are familiar with the data collection methods to be used.

Some examples of objective tests or measures that are appropriate for intergenerational program evaluation are:

—Weekly Test Scores
—California Achievement Test (CAT)
—Bayley Scales of Infant Development (Bayley, 1969)
—Wechsler Adult Intelligence Scale (Wechsler, 1955)

Interviews. Interviewing is one of the more difficult evaluative methods to use, due to the skill required to both administer an interview and to analyze the data collected. The structures of an interview will depend on the skill of the interviewer, and the nature of the data needed. Because of the time involved, this methodology is most often used with a select number of intergenerational participants for whom interviewing is the most appropriate methodology. Interviewing is used when:

—Data are difficult to obtain from participants in any other manner (feelings and attitudes of very young children or very frail elders are examples of such a situation).
—Qualitative data are desired to enrich quantitative data (stories from volunteers describing how their volunteer experience has helped them cope with stress in their lives are examples of such a situation).
—More structured evaluative measures are to be developed, and the interview data will be analyzed for this purpose.

Examples of typical interview questions that are appropriate for diverse participants include:

1. In what way has your volunteering with children contributed to your satisfaction with life? (for senior citizen school volunteers)
2. What have you learned from your senior volunteer about school subjects and about non-school subjects? (for students working on a regular basis with senior citizen volunteers in their classrooms)
3. Why are your visits with teenage volunteers important to you? (for frail elders who have weekly visits with teenage volunteers)
4. Tell me about what you do with your older friend in the child care center or draw a picture that shows me what you do to-

gether (for a young child age 4-6 who interacts weekly with older persons in an early childhood site)

CONCLUSION

Intergenerational programs are on the increase throughout the country, and they assume more significant roles in our communities. As they become more evident and assume more important functions, they need to assume a greater responsibility for assessing their effectiveness and their contribution to the community. Comprehensive evaluations of intergenerational programs are essential to their future growth and success. The direct effect of intergenerational programs on the participants and their indirect effect in the community can become a barometer for their continuation as an entity in the field of human service delivery.

In this paper, we have discussed some of the basic elements to be considered in evaluating intergenerational programs. These elements include:

— the reasons for evaluation,
— the unique features of intergenerational programs that need to be evaluated,
— the strategies involved in conducting an evaluation,
— the components of evaluation data that can be gathered,
— the methodology used to conduct evaluation, and
— some areas in which evaluation outcomes can be reported.

Serious evaluation efforts conducted by intergenerational programs are essential if the programs are to continue to contribute to the quality of life in a community.

The evaluations, therefore, should give insights into:

— the problem areas that typically emerge during the development of intergenerational programs,
— the elements of intergenerational programs that enhance their probability of success,
— the components of intergenerational programs that can be replicated and how this replication can occur,

—the persons in a community who can benefit from intergenerational programs and the nature of these benefits,

—the role of systems and agencies in the creation of successful intergenerational programs, and

—the societal issues that can be addressed through intergenerational programs.

The time spent in the careful preparation and implementation of evaluation procedures for intergenerational programs will result in the improved quality of these programs, in the improved competence of program staff, in the community's understanding of them and in their probable survival as a force for change in the community.

REFERENCES

Bayley, N. (1969). *Bayley Scales of Infant Development*. New York: The Psychological Corporation.

Gurland, B.J., Bennett, R. & Wilder, D. (1984). Reevaluating the place of evaluation in planning for alternatives to institutional care for the elderly. In Bennet, R., Frish, S., Gurland, B.J., & Wilder, D. (Eds.). *Coordinated Service Delivery Systems for the Elderly* (pp. 159-180). New York: Haworth Press.

Mangen, D.J., Bengston, V.L. & Landry Jr., P.H. (1988). *Measurement of intergenerational relations*. Beverly Hills: Sage Publications, Inc.

Hanusa, B., Marks, R., Newman, S. & Onawala, R. (1988). *Modified Children's Views on Aging Questionnaire*. Pittsburgh: Generations Together, University of Pittsburgh.

Neugarten, B., Havighurst, R.J. & Tobin, S. (1961). The measurement of life satisfaction. *Journal of Gerontology, 16*, 134-143.

Newman, S. & Onawola, R. (1986). *Flanders Interaction Analysis and its Adaptation for Intergenerational Programs (OPSCI)*. Unpublished manuscript, available from Generations Together, 811 William Pitt Union, University of Pittsburgh.

Newman, S., Vasudev, J. & Onawala, R. (1985). Older volunteers' perceptions of impacts of volunteering on their psychological well-being. *Journal of Applied Gerontology, 4* (2), 123-127.

Nursing Assessment Observation Log. In Lyons, C. & Newman, S. (1983). *How to Develop an Intergenerational Service-Learning Program at a Nursing Home*. Unpublished manuscript available from Generations Together, 811 William Pitt Union, Pittsburgh, PA 15260.

Osgood, C.E., Suei, G. & Tannenbaum, C.S. (1957). *The measure of meaning*. Urbana: University of Illinois Press.

Patton, M.Q. (1978). *Utilization-focused evaluation*. Beverly Hills: Sage Publications, Inc.

Seefeldt, C., Jantz, R.K., Galper, A. & Serock, K. (1977). Using pictures to explore children's attitude toward the elderly. *The Gerontologist*, *17* (6), 506-512.

Wechsler, D. (1955). *Wechsler adult intelligence scale*. New York: Psychological Corporation.

Linking Systems:
A Systems Approach
to Intergenerational Programming

Nancy Z. Henkin, PhD
Sandra W. Sweeney, MEd

SUMMARY. A systems approach to intergenerational programming involves a structured way of thinking about program development and problem solving. This paper describes the essential components and anticipated outcomes of this process which can be implemented effectively at the local, state and national levels.

BEYOND THE MODEL PROJECT

With the increasing complexity of our lives and the decreasing resources available to meet the needs of young and old, it is critical that communities develop the most efficient and effective organizational strategies to address the challenges that face them. Changing demographics as well as the growing stress on families and their children require new alternatives for meeting human and organizational needs.

Children and older persons share similar and increasingly competitive interests in health, nutrition, and caregiving services as well as the need for education and coping skills to deal with life's difficult transitions. Most intergenerational programs focus on bringing alternate generations together to develop relationships and/or provide service. These activities emphasize the need for emotional in-

Nancy Z. Henkin is affiliated with the Institute on Aging, Temple University, 1601 North Broad Street, Philadelphia, PA 19122. Sandra W. Sweeney is Manager, Special Project Section, American Association of Retired Persons, 1909 K Street, NW, Washington, DC 20049.

terchange and support as well as changed attitudes of one generation for another. Although many innovative programs have been
developed over the past several years, most of these are generally
viable only as long as the individuals who created them maintain
personal interest and responsibility for them.

A new way of looking at intergenerational programming has
emerged in response to the demand to increase effectiveness and
conserve resources. Instead of depending on the interest and motivation of individuals with their own perceptions of service needs,
the systems approach involves a structured way of thinking about
program development and problem solving. Whether the "system"
being addressed is a group of organizations with related goals in a
geographic area, a special population within the community or the
linking of age related organizations, the emphasis is on assessing
the needs of community members and finding intergenerational solutions to gaps in services.

By working together, organizations with seemingly different
goals can maximize their resources while meeting a wider range of
needs in the community. Collaborative programming allows organizations to see the interrelatedness of needs and encourages an integrated approach to problem solving. Through the systems approach, communities can more effectively use their resources and
strengthen their capacity for effective program delivery.

STRATEGIES FOR LINKING SYSTEMS

The effort to link systems can be made on a local, state, or national level. No matter where the linkage is initiated, it is important
to approach the process in a structured and deliberate manner. Either an external catalyst or someone representing one of the systems
involved is needed to spearhead this effort. The following are essential components of the process.

Assessment of Needs

Any attempt to link specific systems in collaborative programming should grow out of a demonstrated need and should be clearly
beneficial to all organizations involved. An overly simplistic diag-

nosis and intervention must be avoided. Since the organizational needs as well as the needs of the youth, elders and families should be considered in a collaborative program, a systematic and comprehensive examination of all problems is essential for successful and sustained program implementation. An overly simplistic approach to this complex effort must be avoided (see Brummel in this edition).

On a local level, a needs assessment may involve gathering information from key leaders in a variety of networks to determine the most pressing problems caused by gaps in service which exist in a community. Interagency task forces can be useful in prioritizing issues and formulating strategies for appropriate interventions to reduce these problems. On a state or national level, an analysis of policies and programs may be required to determine in which area(s) collaborative efforts would be most beneficial.

Raising Awareness

Raising awareness about the benefits accrued from sharing resources through intergenerational programming is critical. Most age-specific organizations are strongly committed to their constituencies and often have a narrow view of their missions. A sophisticated marketing approach is necessary to help participating systems recognize the potential positive outcomes from collaborative program development. Presentations at local, state, and national meetings and effective public relations strategies can generate enthusiasm and encourage the commitment of resources from diversified organizations.

Understanding Each Other's Systems

Whether different systems are brought together by an external catalyst or someone from within one of the participating networks, it is essential that the collaborators understand each other's working context. Information about goals, objectives, resources, program components, management, and internal constraints must be shared in order to insure that a collaborative effort is realistic and has a good chance for success. It is important that individuals from different networks speak a common language, understand each other's operations, and ultimately are able to formulate common goals.

Clarifying Goals and Roles

After the leaders of each system have made a commitment to the development of a collaborative program, the goals of the program and the roles of the participating agencies must be clarified. Developing an informal contract or memorandum of understanding can help to promote a positive working arrangement.

One of the most serious barriers to the success of collaborative programs is the "turf issue." Age-segregated policies and funding streams exacerbated by a decrease in government funding have created a situation in which competition between constituent groups is expected and accepted. On both a national and local level, the "gray" lobby competes with the children's lobby for scarce resources. Anxious to protect what they have, leaders of both aging and youth organizations rarely view collaborative efforts as a viable way of maximizing resources. Turf issues often remain unresolved and undermine the entire process.

A second problem related to role clarification involves the issue of "ownership" when an outside catalyst is involved. The degree to which the catalyst is involved and/or assumes direct leadership varies depending on the scope of the programs being planned and the skills of the program developers. Finding an effective balance between direct intervention and indirect facilitation is often quite difficult.

Training and Technical Assistance

For any collaborative effort to succeed, orientation for top administrators and "hands on" training for practitioners must be an integral part of the program. Often staff are resistant to new initiatives, particularly those involving other constituency groups. Training should address both attitudinal issues and specific skill-building techniques (see Vander Ven in this publication). It should be designed in a way that builds upon the strengths and resources of each system and encourages interdependence among the participating organizations.

If technical assistance is provided by an external catalyst, the development of a relationship based on trust must be established early. Often organizations are unaccustomed to the availability of a technical consultant and are reluctant to call upon one. Altering this "mind-set" and encouraging organizations to ask for assistance is part of the external catalyst's role.

Evaluation and Information Dissemination

An evaluation of the degree to which intergenerational projects are successful in meeting their objectives as well as the total impact of the effort on the systems involved is critical (see Bocian & Newman in this edition). Results should be disseminated widely through the appropriate networks. Evaluation data can be used to garner more commitment from the participating networks as well as funding from private and public sources.

SOME EXAMPLES

Although the systems approach to intergenerational programming is complex, there are a growing number of such efforts across the country. An example of a local community effort is the Delaware Valley Intergenerational Network (DELVIN). DELVIN was created in 1985 to bring together the education, aging, youth services, religious, voluntary, and child care networks in Philadelphia and the surrounding four counties. In each county, an intergenerational task force has been created to prioritize community needs and identify gaps in service delivery. Telephone reassurance programs involving homebound elders calling latchkey children; oral history projects at neighborhood libraries; elders assisting troubled families; "caring block" projects in settlement houses and many other activities have grown out of this intensive effort. Coordinated by the Center for Intergenerational Learning at Temple University's Institute on Aging, DELVIN is funded by area foundations and corporations. In addition to the five county task forces, conferences and training workshops are conducted to raise awareness about the range of potential programs and to help program developers enhance their skills. A quarterly newsletter is published and widely disseminated throughout Delaware Valley.

In Illinois, a coalition of 40 education, aging, and volunteer agencies have organized and drafted a state model for "involving older adults in education." Funded by the Illinois Board of Higher Education, the project began in 1985 at an invitational conference which brought together key organizers and decision makers to formulate a statewide intergenerational program initiative. The major program areas addressed by the state model included the development of intergenerational programs in pre-kindergarten through graduate levels in all Illinois schools. Their five year goal is to make the involvement of older adults in education the *rule* rather than the exception.

On a national level, Generations United: A National Coalition in Intergenerational Issues and Programs was formed in 1986. Through education, public policy efforts, and dissemination of programmatic information, this coalition of over 100 non-profit organizations seeks to foster greater intergenerational harmony and serve as an advocate for all generations.

BENEFITS

Often the initiators of programs choose the short-term rewards of program implementation over the long-term advantages of stimulating fundamental change in systems. Collaborative projects, while more difficult to achieve, have long lasting effects on individuals and systems. While individual intergenerational programs of all kinds provide opportunities for valuable relationships between young and old, there are special and more permanent benefits that accrue to programs which take a broader approach to planning and development.

COST-EFFECTIVENESS

Programs which combine the efforts of organizations with vested interest in finding cooperative solutions are often more cost-effective than single agency programs. The competition for resources is diffused and the cooperative use of human and service resources as well as funds results in a multiplier effect. Several organizations contribute to the whole rather than one agency sustaining the entire effort. Each agency is able to contribute from its existing service strengths rather than straining already overused resources. Where programs may have competed for volunteers with similar skills and interests, they can now recruit those most able for their joint effort. This is a particularly important advantage in times of limited resources.

ORGANIZATIONAL EFFECTIVENESS

Involving systems in collaborative program development can have long-term effects on the attitudes and operation of the organizations themselves. Designing programs to meet system needs requires organizational staff to expand their perspective beyond individual constituent groups and assess community problems more broadly. In addition, collaborative projects require careful planning, a skill that is basic to successful programming. Good programs born of cooperative planning encourage programmers to use this valuable process in continuing needs identification and problem solving. Furthermore, a belief in the collaborative process strengthens the ability of systems to marshal their resources and of the community to meet its needs.

REPLICATION AND LONG-TERM SURVIVAL

When programs are developed in the context of collaboration between existing community institutions, the possibility for replication is enhanced.

Often individual community agencies are part of a larger state or national system. Involving these agencies in collaborative program development often results in models that can be easily replicated in other communities which share common needs. Institutions may reject program ideas which have no apparent connection to their goals, giving needs-based programs a greater opportunity for survival and replication.

Programs, therefore, which are developed as a response to real and recognized needs of a community are more likely to appeal to the interests of a wide range of organizations. When agencies begin to see the program as valuable in meeting their goals, the program concept has a greater chance for integration in the mission of the system and, therefore, a greater chance for survival as an integral part of the service goals. In addition to the advantages experienced in implementing programs themselves, there are benefits experienced by the community as a whole. Traditional intergenerational activities focus on building relationships between young and old, dispelling stereotypes and changing attitudes. Programs which, in addition, seek solutions to community problems can focus the resources of systems and organizations on intergenerational solutions to the substantive needs of families and communities. With this approach, the goal is to build the capacity of systems to meet the needs of various age groups through collaboration. Emphasizing interagency and community problem solving rather than individual benefits invites community investment in the program and a cohesiveness built upon the involvement of people across generations.

The benefits of involving the community and its systems in assessing community needs and finding appropriate intergenerational solutions are many. The development of intergenerational programs in the broader context of cooperative planning enhances the possibility for program effectiveness, survival and replication. The attention to community needs invites greater overall community support and an understanding of the power of collaborative problem solving. The systems approach allows organizations to address issues related to an organizational mission while ensuring a long-range commitment to solving the problems of multiple organizations and the generations they serve.

REFERENCES

Allen, J. & Lientz, B. (1978). *Systems in action: A managerial and social approach*. Santa Monica, CA: Goodyear Publishing.

Ventura-Merkel, C. & Ledoff, L. (1983). *Program innovation in aging: Volume VIII, community planning for intergenerational programming*. Washington, DC: National Council on the Aging, Inc.

Exemplary Intergenerational Programs

Catherine Ventura-Merkel, MGS
David S. Liederman, MSW
Jack Ossofsky

SUMMARY. In times of shrinking resources and growing needs, service providers of the young and the old must work together to increase intergenerational cooperation and exchange through programs which can most effectively and efficiently meet the needs of persons from all social and economic walks of life. Successful and exemplary intergenerational programs appear to have numerous similar characteristics that set them apart from others — they address major social issues or problems, rebuild natural helping relationships, are mutually supportive and beneficial to all generations involved, provide optimum use of financial resources, build on existing services of institutions and provide opportunities for communities to design programs appropriate to local needs. Such exemplary intergenerational programs can be found in almost all areas of human services. This paper discusses the characteristics of exemplary intergenerational programs as well as program models addressing a variety of needs, serving many different populations and representing creative responses to a range of community problems.

Not too long ago, people were asking: What is intergenerational programming? Why are such programs necessary? What needs do they meet? Why would older and younger persons want to come together? Who benefits?

To address these very basic questions, interested persons were

Catherine Ventura-Merkel is NCOA Program Associate and Generations United Project Coordinator, David S. Liederman is Executive Director of the Child Welfare League of America and Generations United Co-Chair, and Jack Ossofsky is President, The National Council on the Aging, and Generations United Co-Chair, 600 Maryland Avenue, SW, West Wing 100, Washington, DC 20024.

referred to program descriptions, directories and catalogues of pro-files (Murphy, 1984; Ventura-Merkel & Parks, 1984). These guides were designed to share information and program ideas, but were inadequate in addressing basic programmatic and evaluative issues.

The compilation of papers in this publication shows that we have moved from these basic questions to a more sophisticated level of thinking about intergenerational programming. We are now faced with questions regarding: What should be considered exemplary in the area of intergenerational programming? What models of exem-plary programs are currently available?

We invite this opportunity to reflect on these questions and are eager to suggest characteristics and models of exemplary intergen-erational programs. In both the fields of aging and child welfare, we seek to develop programs which can most effectively and efficiently meet the needs of persons from all social and economic walks of life. It was this common desire—to find creative ways of serving both young and old—that initially brought us together and which resulted in the formation of Generations United: A National Coali-tion on Intergenerational Issues and Programs, a group of more than 100 national organizations that seeks to promote intergenerational cooperation and exchange through uniting on public policy and pro-gramming efforts.

WHAT TYPES OF PROGRAMS EXIST?

Generations United defines intergenerational programming as the purposeful bringing together of different generations in ongoing planned activities designed to achieve the development of new rela-tionships as well as specified program goals. Most often, programs focus on bringing together youth age 25 and younger and older persons age 60 and over, but it also concerns the middle generation, the "sandwich" generation, faced with caring for the dependent children as well as aging parents.

Hundreds, perhaps thousands, of intergenerational programs have been initiated in the past decade. The settings for these pro-grams are as varied as the populations they serve, and include: child and adult day care centers, elementary and secondary schools, youth shelters, colleges and universities, senior centers, senior residences, hospitals, nursing homes, foster care homes and churches. Programs have been successful in both home and professional environments, serving needs of all age groups and addressing a wide range of problems.

Some programs are aimed at providing fun and friendship, and others toward complex educational or service components. But the bottom line is always the same: bringing people together from different generations who might not normally have access to such relationships and enabling them to benefit and learn from each other.

SUCCESSFUL AND EXEMPLARY INTERGENERATIONAL PROGRAMS

Within the wider sweep of intergenerational programming is a smaller, but also growing, number of initiatives that might be considered exemplary. By exemplary, we mean worthy of being replicated or copied. Many of these programs share several common characteristics which have contributed to their success.

In 1985, Henkin and Newman listed the following as some of the characteristics of successful intergenerational programs:

— clearly defined goals and objectives
— supportive administrative and programmatic staff
— collaboration between the systems or agencies representing the younger and older participants
— competent and committed program leadership
— well-trained and committed staff
— sensitivity to the needs and expectations of the participants (young and old, professional and volunteer)
— a program of manageable size
— consistent and meaningful recognition for volunteers and professional participants
— ongoing evaluation procedures

In identifying exemplary program models, we believe there are additional criteria or factors of a broader, more qualitative and subjective nature that should be considered.

An exemplary intergenerational program should:

—Address a major social problem or issue. The major significance of the evolution of intergenerational programming is based on the fact that they *can* address major social issues, particularly by meeting critical needs of vulnerable or disadvantaged population. Intergenerational programs serve at-risk children and youth, including pregnant teenagers, incarcerated youth and young adults, substance abusers, abused children and chronically ill and disabled children; they reach out to socially isolated elderly or help middle-aged caregivers cope with their aging parents; they provide role models for altruism and idealism and they provide important employment and volunteer opportunities for young and old.

—Rebuild the natural helping relationships that were once provided by extended families and neighborhoods. The advent of an aging society and dramatic changes in family structure have increased the social separation and isolation of the generations. Intergenerational programs can provide a renewed sense of community and continuity by reminding people of diverse ages, interests and backgrounds that the community is an interdependent environment that relies on a delicate balance among all segments of the population.

—Be mutually supportive and beneficial to all generations involved, not exploiting one generation or the other. In order to reduce stereotypes and to promote mutual respect, all participants must give as well as receive.

—Provide optimum use of financial resources in communities. Because intergenerational programs often require the sharing of limited resources, they are almost always cost-effective, making optimal use of whatever is available.

—Build on existing services of institutions. Rather than simply developing programs and services to address every existing or new problem, intergenerational methods and strategies can build on existing services and institutions.

—Provide opportunities for local communities to design, support and maintain programs that are appropriate to local resources and needs. Just as a family must rely on cooperation, trust and interdependent values to make difficult decisions about dwindling resources to meet the needs of children and aging parents, so too must a community learn to work in cooperation with a new set of interdependent values to support the well-being of all citizens.

EXEMPLARY INTERGENERATIONAL PROGRAMS

The following discussion of exemplary intergenerational programs generically describes programs that we know have been successful and basically meet the criteria described previously. An extended effort was made not to describe specific programs but, rather, to provide an overview of exemplary programs, ideas and models.

Child Day Care Centers Staffed by Older Workers and Volunteers. Child care centers offering services to the young child (infants to preschoolers) provide working parents with a badly needed service, provide intergenerational contact and stimulation between young and old, and provide supplemental income opportunities for older workers.

Child Care Centers in Long-Term Care Facilities. These centers combine a variety of resources in facilities for young and old. In many instances, the child service is for employees of the long-term care facility; in others, the service is open in the community. The intergenerational interaction between the residents and children is usually planned, although spontaneous interaction has proven effective as well.

Adult Day Care and Child Day Care Offered in the Same Facility. Adult day care programs and child day care programs are housed in the same facility, and participate in numerous joint activities. Each has its own staff and space so that the special needs of each population can be met.

Trained Older Workers as Family Day Care Providers. Using job training partnership funding (JTPA) and Title V Workers, some community colleges are training older workers as family day care providers. The older workers are then certified to provide child day care in their homes, offering them new sources of income and the opportunity to develop new roles and relationships.

Latchkey Projects. A number of intergenerational projects have been developed to meet the needs of school-age children and working parents. Examples of some projects include: a senior center latchkey model in which children in nearby schools attend a planned after-school program at a local senior center; after-school programs staffed by older workers which take place in the schools or at other community sites; telephone reassurance programs, also called intergenerational hotlines, in which older volunteers are regularly in touch with latchkey children when they return home after school to an empty house.

Older School Volunteer Programs. Many school systems have volunteer programs, and many have learned to utilize older volunteers as a resource. The skills and interests of the older adults are matched with the needs of the school/teachers. Some of the many basic ways older school volunteers help in schools are: tutoring, enrichment activities, classroom teaching aides, librarian assistants, teaching about aging and the aging process, and living/oral historians.

Child Welfare Programs. Many older persons play supportive roles in relationships with children and youth who are "vulnerable." For many, that vulnerability is the result of abuse or neglect they have suffered—and which continue to pose a threat for the future. For others, their vulnerability stems from teen pregnancy, encounters with the juvenile justice system, from dropping out of school or being unemployed. In an attempt to help these young victims, often living in poverty, intergenerational programs are drawing on the parenting and life experience of older adults to help foster families cope with the needs of the foster children, assist the natural families of foster children with the transition from foster care back to home, assist child abusers in learning new ways to cope with the stresses and demands of parenting, and help teenage mothers raise their children and continue their schooling. Other such initiatives are working with juvenile offenders to keep them out of jail or provide support during incarceration. Elsewhere, programs are drawing on the skills of retirees to strengthen the employment prospects of disadvantaged youth. These programs range from more established efforts such as federally funded Foster Grandparent programs to unique projects pulled together at the grassroots levels.

Life Enrichment. Many groups of young and old have found a common ground through intergenerational programs dealing with the arts and humanities. In hundreds of instances, across the country, old and young come together to share common experiences. They form intergenerational dance and theater groups and choruses and orchestras. Senior centers and schools collaborate on developing local history projects that result in publications and exhibits. Discussion groups of young and old share in the study of literature or the Constitution. In other programs, principally designed for older persons teaching their arts to the young as mentors, the lifetime experiences of the older persons provide a wealth of artistic knowledge and skill to share with and pass on to succeeding generations.

Service Programs to Frail and Homebound Elderly. Many older persons are trying to remain in their own homes and communities, maintaining their independence and their health, despite the physical, social and economic changes which they may be experiencing. Numerous intergenerational programs bring together the needs of frail and homebound older persons and service opportunities for youth. In several programs across the country, young people provide a range of services to this population including friendly visiting, chore services, seasonal yard work, home repair, escort and transportation service and companionship. One variation of this type of program includes the participation of older workers as managers of designated services, such as home repair, as instructors for young student workers or as co-workers. This model creates a unique experience for youth enabling them to work with both the frail and healthy older person. Service programs to frail and homebound elderly will become increasingly important as older persons are discharged from hospitals more quickly than in the past and in need of more assistance.

CONCLUSION

We could continue this presentation of exemplary intergenerational programs with a discussion of intergenerational programs in other settings, meeting the needs of other populations, providing different services, and representing creative responses to pressing community problems. However, our mission was to provide a sampling of what is in place and to provide a sense of the range of options possible. The ideas presented are intended to serve as representative of variations which we believe can be adapted or replicated.

While no substitute for family support or compensation for cutbacks in government resources for needy older Americans and youth, intergenerational programs nevertheless hold enormous promise for helping some of society's most vulnerable citizens. The potential importance of the supportive one-to-one relationships these programs foster and the learning that is exchanged by older and younger participants is considerable. While much research is needed to determine the impact of intergenerational programs, the exemplary and successful programs that exist make a compelling case for their continued growth and establishment.

REFERENCES

Henkin, N.Z. & Newman, S.M. (1985). *The best of you . . . the best of me: An instructional guide*. Harrisburg: The Commonwealth of Pennsylvania Department of Aging.

Murphy, M.B. (1984). *A guide to intergenerational programming*. Washington, DC: National Association of State Units on Aging.

Ventura-Merkel, C. & Parks, E. (1984). *Intergenerational programs: A catalogue of profiles*. Washington, DC: National Council on the Aging, Inc.

PART III:
IMPACTS

Introduction

Currently, the research data available on intergenerational programs reports on two aspects of program impact related to the older and younger participants: attitudes and quality of life. This data is substantial and has validated and verified the effectiveness of these programs. There is a need, however, to address additional aspects of intergenerational program efforts in relationship to the imperatives that seem to justify their timeliness. Part III presents papers that report on the current research and establishes some of the issues related to future research efforts.

Carol Seefeldt in "Intergenerational Programs — Impact on Attitudes" reports survey results of young and old participants in intergenerational programs. She indicates that though older people look most favorably on their intergenerational experience, the reports from younger participants are mixed and are often related to the level of functioning of the older person with whom the youth are interacting. Norman L. Proller in "The Effects of an Adoptive Grandparent Program on Youth and Elderly Participants" discusses the results of a study to determine the effect of intergenerational exchange on 5th and 6th grade students and residents of a nursing home. Rosalyn Saltz in "Research Evaluation of a Foster Grandparent Program," describes the results of a longitudinal research paper that evaluated the effect of the Detroit Foster Grandparent Program on the personal development of the elder participants.

In his paper "Intergenerational Program Research to Refine Theory and Practice," Donald Cohon presents several theories that provide the rationale for undertaking intergenerational programming and exchange and upon which intergenerational research concepts are based. A number of recent studies are reviewed and the implications for future research are outlined.

Sally Newman, PhD
Steven W. Brummel, MA

183

Intergenerational Programs — Impact on Attitudes

Carol Seefeldt, PhD

SUMMARY. This paper reports on the impact on attitudes of younger and older participants in intergenerational programs. The elderly surveyed in several programs reported increased feelings of well-being and life-satisfaction as a result of their involvement with children. The results from children, however, are mixed with both positive and negative attitudinal outcomes attributed to their intergenerational experiences. The author suggests that measuring attitude change might be more conclusive if the research considered the longitudinal growth and development associated with attitude learning and change.

It's a popular idea; on "St. Elsewhere" an elderly woman finds security by becoming a foster grandparent in the children's ward. Newspapers feature photos of children being cared for by elders. Images of the young and old interacting, sharing and caring for one another create heartwarming feelings in each of us.

There is more to the picture of young and old together than stirring, emotional feelings. For our society to continue, children and elderly must have contact with one another. "The continuity of all cultures depends on the living presence of at least three generations" wrote Margaret Mead (1970). Because the natural ways the old and young used to interact, share with and care for one another are disappearing in our society, new ways are being found to provide the "living presence" of three generations for today's children.

Carol Seefeldt is Professor of Education, Institute for Child Study, College of Education, University of Maryland, College Park, MD 20742.

INTERGENERATIONAL PROGRAMS

One way of restoring the caring connections between old and young is through the creation of intergenerational programs. Intergenerational programs may be sponsored by a variety of agencies and take many forms. They typically, however, share common goals of recreating the once natural connections between old and young, and fostering positive attitudes between the young and old.

School systems and child care programs sponsor many of these intergenerational programs. In Memphis, Tennessee, a day care center called Grammas is staffed entirely with older adults. The Generations Together Program in Western Pennsylvania provides senior volunteers to 23 school districts; in San Francisco, Senior Enriching Educational Roles offers resource persons to talk and work with students in career planning; and in Binghamton, New York, the Intergenerational Activities Program of the Broome County Child Development Council links preschool children with frail elderly in a long-term care institution. Throughout the nation the Retired Senior Volunteer Program provides older volunteers to school systems.

Intergenerational programs are not only found in schools or child care programs. They may be sponsored by and located in libraries, museums, on tennis courts, jails, churches or "on common ground" as in a program in which young and old work together cultivating gardens.

INTERGENERATIONAL PROGRAMS
BENEFIT ELDERS

Regardless of sponsor, program type or location, intergenerational programs are believed to be beneficial. The old are believed to benefit from contact with the young. Feelings of improved self-esteem and life-satisfaction that result as they watch children grow and develop. Actually observing the results of their work as children grow and learn, elders see the difference they make in the lives of children. "It's better than any medicine" reported an older woman working in a child care center (Whitely, Duncan, McKenzie, & Sledjeski, 1976). "Being with the children makes me feel alive again. I know they need me, but I need them too," claimed another volunteer.

Research supports these opinions. Higgans and Faunce (1977) surveyed 260 senior citizens and 529 fifth graders in order to determine how they felt about each other and how they perceived each other. The findings showed that, in general, the young and old had favorable feelings toward each other. These feelings were not dependent on the amount of contact between generations.

In a nation-wide survey, people over 70 years of age reported that they enjoyed being in the company of children (Seefeldt, 1982). This group of elders responded that children would make good friends for older people. The old expressed acceptance of children and thought that they would find things to do together that would bring mutual enjoyment and satisfaction. After all, one older woman wrote, "Children are the hope of the future, the joy of one's life. Being with them keeps me focused on tomorrow."

Elders who participated in a program working as foster grandparents with retarded children expressed greater personal and social adjustment and life satisfaction than those elders who had not participated in the program (Gray & Kasteler, 1970). Final reports from The Teaching-Learning Communities (Tice, 1980) also show that elders, as volunteers in a school setting, enjoy their work with children and believe this experience contributes to increased feelings of well-being and life-satisfaction.

Elders' attitudes toward children did not change on an objective measure after participation in a tutorial intergenerational program. On the other hand, this group of elders reported that they were happier and felt more involved in the community as a result of working in the intergenerational program. "Consistent interaction between young and old in intergenerational school programs," writes Newman, "improves older persons' feelings of life satisfaction and children's academic and social growth and attitudes toward the elderly" (Newman, 1985, p. 24).

INTERGENERATIONAL PROGRAMS BENEFIT CHILDREN

Intergenerational programs are thought to benefit children too. However, prior to involvement in these programs, children seem to possess a negative attitude toward aging and the old (Tuckerman & Lorge, 1953; Lane, 1963; Kastenbaum & Durkee, 1964; Hickey & Kalish, 1968). "They have all wrinkled up faces and no hair," reported a fourth grade child. "No, I don't want to grow old. The joy of life will be gone," said another. "Oh, no, not me! I don't ever want to grow old — that's being sick, ugly and tired" stated some of the children in a study exploring 3- to 11-year-old children's attitudes toward the elderly (Jantz, Seefeldt, Galper, & Serock, 1977).

Research theory suggests that it is easier for children to believe in myths about a group of people and accept stereotypes about the group if they have no contact with that group. Because of children's lack of contact with elders, and their overall generally negative attitudes toward aging and the elders, a common goal of intergenerational programs is to foster positive attitudes toward age and the old. Parnell (1980) in a review of the impact on intergenerational programs reached the conclusion that children do appear to develop a more realistic understanding of the aging process and change some of their negative thinking about the elderly as a result of participation in an intergenerational program.

"They love me. I can sit on their lap and they tell me stories about the old days." "They always have time for me. My Grandma Kate never says hurry up." Children often express positive feelings toward old people. They enjoy the intergenerational experience.

Studies document other benefits of intergenerational programs for children. After participation in a curriculum that included contact with active older persons, children in a nursery school through the third grade evaluated old people more positively than before the participation (Seefeldt, Jantz, Galper, & Serock, 1979). Contact with elders was also believed responsible for positive attitude change toward the elderly in a sample of grade school children reported by Rosencranz and McNevin (1969).

Kocarnik and Ponzetti (1986) investigated the effect of children under the age of 5 visiting elderly residents in a nursing home on a continuing basis. The children were interviewed individually and shown photographs of females classified as young, middle-aged, and elderly. The conclusion was that contact, through the intergenerational nursing home program, did result in children evaluating the elderly in more positive ways. The more familiar the children were with each elderly woman, the more positive was their evaluation of older people in general.

Increased contact with elders in a nursing home also appeared to be related to positive attitude change in a group of sixth graders (Allred, Gladeen & Dobson, 1987).

Classroom interaction with older people, along with exposure to media and the presentation of accurate information about aging, was positively related to changes in preschoolers' attitudes toward aging and the elderly (Dellmann-Jenkins, 1986). In addition to being with older people, these children were asked to discuss themes such as "When I grow up" and think about what they would be like when they were old.

Other studies document the success of intergenerational programs in fostering positive attitudes toward the old. Glass and Trent (1980) report improved attitudes toward the elderly as an outcome of 4-H Club activities involving older people. Campi (1984) attributed more positive attitudes toward the elderly to an increase in intergenerational contact.

Young students who participated in a curriculum providing them with reliable data and information about the elderly, as well as contact with older persons, were found to increase their accuracy of knowledge of old people and the process of aging (Sorgam, Margo & Sorensen, 1984). Learning to view the world as a global village, developing the concept of interdependence not only of cultures and countries but also of generations, was believed to enable young people to give up stereotypes about age and the elderly (Ulin, 1982).

With the goal of providing accurate information about the elderly, an inquiry lesson on aging was implemented in the intermediate grades by Laney (1987). The goals were to provide accurate information about the elderly. Following the curriculum, children were better able to assess their own perceptions about the aging process, and they were able to give an unbiased response of the attributes, behavior, and characteristics of the elderly.

Structured intergenerational dialogues by older volunteers and 10- to 11-year-old students were arranged as a part of an educational program. The data indicated that this experience resulted in an increase in understanding issues related to aging as well as to an increase in knowledge of older persons.

INTERGENERATIONAL PROGRAMS
WITHOUT BENEFITS

Not all intergenerational programs are able to document positive changes in children's or elders' attitudes toward one another, nor do all lead to an increase in self-esteem and life-satisfaction on the part of elders. Ivester and King (1977) found no association between contact with grandparents and positive attitudes toward the elderly. Drake (1957) concluded that undergraduate students who maintained contact with their grandparents scored no differently than those without the contact on the Tuckerman-Lorge questionnaire of attitudes toward the elderly.

Lessons on death and dying designed to change adolescents' attitudes toward older adults did not appear to be effective. In this study, high school students participated in a two week study of aging, death and dying. A variety of experiences, including contact with older persons was included. The children did experience a small decrease in death anxiety. On the other hand, their attitudes toward the old became more negative (Glass & Knott, 1984). Long (1983) also found that contact with old people did not change negative attitudes toward aging and the elderly. In this study, the effects of older persons as students in undergraduate classes was assessed on social relations and attitudes toward the elderly. Those students who experienced the intergenerational classrooms supported the concept, yet their attitudes toward aging and the elderly did not change.

Mixed results on the impact of intergenerational contact are reported by other researchers. Seefeldt and Jantz (1977) concluded that children from kindergarten through the sixth grade were less likely to stereotype elders on the basis of physical or behavioral characteristics following contact with older adults in a school setting. This group, however, retained strong negative attitudes toward their own aging. Olejnik and LaRue (1981) found that middle school children, following eating lunch with elders over a period of 2 months, were more positive in rating the physical and security aspects of aging, yet were less likely to want to be with elders following the contact.

Some studies report negative results after participation in intergenerational programs. Baggett (1981) found that a group of children from kindergarten through the third grade responded more negatively to an attitude measure following experiences with elders than children without this experience. Following participation in the program "Off the Rocker" children rated elders as less active than did children without the experience (1981). Immorlica (1980) found that the greater the intergenerational interactions between elder volunteers and 120 elementary school children, the more unfavorable were children's attitudes toward the elderly.

When children under the age of 5 were taken weekly to visit infirm elders in a nursing home setting, their attitudes toward their own aging and the elderly were more negative than children without the experience. Although the staff of both the child care program and the nursing home believed the experience was beneficial for children and patients, 90% of the 30 children randomly selected for weekly visits to the nursing home reported they would feel "bad" when they were old. This group also rated the young as helpful, healthier, friendlier, happier and better than old people.

MAKING SURE INTERGENERATIONAL PROGRAMS WORK

Intergenerational programs are definitely here to stay. They are popular with the public. Good feelings and emotions accompany them. And by and large, the programs do appear to work in achieving goals of building continuity between generations, fostering positive intergenerational attitudes and benefiting both children and elders.

Nevertheless, in order to assure the success and continuation of intergenerational programs, care is needed in evaluating and documenting how intergenerational contact does impact on children, elders and the program.

It is important for all programs to be able to clearly articulate their goals and objectives and then document how these have been achieved. Objective measures, standardized testing procedures and statistical analysis are necessary accountability tools. These are, however, only one form of documenting success.

Different forms of observations can be used to describe program success in addition to statistical analysis. For instance, in Project Caressing, elder volunteers caress, rock, hold, stroke and soothe infants and toddlers from two months to two years old. The confidence, trust and bonding believed to result from this experience for the children cannot be measured with standardized tests. The response of the infants and toddlers, their smiles, coos, reaching out to others, however, can be described in anecdotes, candid photos or videotapes. The reactions of the volunteers, as well, need to be recorded.

In another intergenerational program in a battered women's shelter, the goal of the older volunteer is to give one-on-one attention to children in the center. As the children may or may not return, there is no way to follow up or measure the impact of the contact. The type of one-on-one attention given to children in this center can only be measured through description or observation.

Asking the elders, and children, to write a journal about their experiences, taking videotapes, informal photos, and always recording observations, provide data to support the continuation and expansion of intergenerational programs.

Outcomes other than change in attitudes toward old and young can be considered in evaluation. Programs could demonstrate the cost effectiveness of an intergenerational program or show how the program benefits staff, parents and others involved. Variables such as attendance in the program, numbers of articles in the local newspaper, public awareness or others could be assessed and used as evidence in support of intergenerational programs.

CONCLUSION

As the first stage of attitude change resulting from contact with another group is often a negative one (Amir, 1969), it might be effective to measure attitude change on a continuing and long-term basis rather than only on the pre-post test model. To say that attitudes toward elders or children do change in either direction after contact, research does not address the longitudinal growth and development associated with attitude learning and change.

If we do believe that "the joining of the young and old can be a mutually happy experience" (McDuffie, 1986, p. 45) then we, as a society, can carefully and thoughtfully plan and implement intergenerational programs; programs that are planned and evaluated with equal attentiveness.

REFERENCES

Amir, T. (1969). Contact hypothesis in ethnic relations. *Psychological Bulletin, 71*, 319-342.

Allred, G.B. & Dobson, J.E. (1987). Remotivation group interaction: Increasing children's contact with the elderly. *Elementary School Guidance and Counseling, 21*, 216-220.

Baggett, S. (1981). Attitudinal consequences of older adult volunteers in the public school setting. *Educational Gerontology, 7*(3), 21-31.

Caspi, A. (1984). Contact hypothesis and inter-age attitudes: A field study of cross-age contact. *Social Psychology Quarterly, 47*, 74-80.

Chappell, G. (1977). The effect of frequent ongoing contact with an old person on young people's attitudes toward the elderly (Doctoral dissertation, The American University). *Dissertation Abstracts International, 38*, 28508.

Dellmann-Jenkins, M. (1986). Old and young together: Effect of an educational program on preschoolers. *Childhood Education, 62*, 206-208.

Drake, J.T. (1957). Some factors influencing students' attitudes toward old people. *Social Forces, 35*, 266-271.

Glass, J.C. & Trent, C. (1980, December). Changing ninth-graders' attitudes toward older persons. *Research on Aging, 2*(4), pp. 499-512.

Gray, R.M. & Kasteler, J.M. (1970). An evaluation of the effectiveness of a foster grandparent project. *Sociology and Social Research, 54*, 181-189.

Hickey, T. & Kalish, R.A. (1968). Young people's perceptions of adults. *Journal of Gerontology, 23*, 215-220.

Higgans, P.S. & Faunce, R. (1977, March). *Attitudes of Minneapolis elementary school students and senior citizens toward each other* (Report no. C-76-34). Minneapolis: Minneapolis Public Schools, Department of Research and Evaluation. (ERIC document reproduction services no. 139 823)

Immorlica, A.C. (1980). The effect of intergenerational contact on children's perceptions of old people (Doctoral dissertation, University of South Carolina). *Dissertation Abstracts International, 40*, 5621B.

Ivester, C. & King, K. (1977). Attitudes toward aging and toward the needs of older people. *Journal of Gerontology, 31*, 5816-594.

Jantz, R.K., Seefeldt, C., Galper, A. & Serock, K. (1977). Children's attitudes toward the elderly. *Social Education, 41*, 518-523.

Kastenbaum, R. & Drukee, N. (1964). Young people view old age. In R. Kastenbaum (Ed.), *New Thoughts on Old Age.* New York: Springer.

Kocarnik, R. & Ponzetti, J.J. (1986). The influence of intergenerational contact on child care participants. *Child Care Quarterly, 15*, 244-250.

Lane, B. (1964). Attitudes of youth toward the aged. *Journal of Marriage and the Family, 36,* 229-231.

Laney, J.D. (1987). Learning about aging: A planned inquiry for intermediate grades. *Social Education, 51,* 269-272.

Mead, M. (1970). *Culture and commitment.* New York: Natural History Museum.

Newman, S. (1985). The impact of intergenerational programs on children's growth and older persons' life satisfaction. In K.A. Struntz & S. Reville (Eds.), *Growing together: An intergenerational sourcebook.* Washington, DC: American Association of Retired Persons; Palm Springs, CA: The Elvirita Lewis Foundation.

Parnell, K. (1980). Young and old together: A literature review. *Childhood Education, 56,* 184-188.

Ric, P.E. (1983). Children's perceptions of the elderly. *Educational Gerontology, 9,* 483-491.

Rosencranz, H.A. & McNevin, T.E. (1969). A factor analysis of attitudes toward the aged. *The Gerontologist, 9*(1), pp. 55-59.

Seefeldt, C. (1982). How elders view children. *Children Today, 11*(2), 16-21.

Seefeldt, C., Jantz, R.K., Galper, S. & Serock, K. (1979). Children's attitudes toward the elderly: Curriculum implications. *Educational Gerontology, 2,* 301-311.

Sheehan, R. (1981). Young children's contact with the elderly. *Journal of Gerontology, 36,* 567-574.

Sorgam, M.I. & Sorensen, M. (1984). Ageism: A course of study. *Theory Into Practice, 23,* 117-123.

Tice, C. (1980). *Teaching-learning communities.* Ann Arbor, MI: Teaching-Learning Communities.

Tuckerman, J. & Lorge, I. (1953). Perceptual stereotypes about life adjustment. *Journal of Social Psychology, 43,* 239-245.

Ulin, R.O. (1982). Aging education in the public schools: A global perspective. *Educational Gerontology, 8,* 537-544.

Whitley, E., Duncan, R., McKenzie, P. & Sledjeski, S. (1976). *From time to time: A record of young children's relationships with aged.* (Research monograph No 17) Gainesville: University of Florida, P.K. Yonge Laboratory School. (ERIC Document Reproduction Service No. ED 128 088)

The Effects of an Adoptive Grandparent Program on Youth and Elderly Participants

Norman L. Proller, PhD

SUMMARY. In this paper, the author describes a quasi-experimental study conducted as part of an evaluation program of the Dade County Public Schools' Adoptive Grandparent Program. The study involved the participation of selected 5th and 6th grade students and residents of a nursing home. It was designed to determine the extent to which involvement in the program influenced the pupils' sense of self-esteem, and their attitude toward the elderly, as well as the elderly's level of depression, self-esteem and attitudes toward aging.

BACKGROUND

The Dade County Public Schools (DCPS) Adoptive Grandparent Program (AGP) has been operating since 1983. It was instituted by an elementary school principal after he heard about a similar program created by staff at the P. K. Yonge School (located in Gainesville, Florida). According to the principal, he developed the program for two basic reasons. First, he discovered that many residents in a nearby residential care facility had few, if any, visitors. Secondly, he learned that numerous 4th, 5th and 6th grade students in his school had little or no contact with elderly individuals. Their families had moved to Miami from other geographical locations, leaving behind their grandparents and other elderly relatives.

His initial program proved most successful as both the residents and the involved pupils spoke very positively about their experiences. Through interviews with the elderly, it was learned that they

---

Norman L. Proller is Assistant Supervisor, Department of Program Evaluation, Office of Educational Accountability, Dade County Public Schools, 1450 North East 2nd Avenue, Miami, FL 33132.

195

"loved" having visits with young children and eagerly looked forward to them. Others added that the visits gave them "something to live for." Comments by some of the youngsters included the fact that they enjoyed learning many things about what life was like in Florida and in the United States, in general, prior to their birth. Interestingly, one particular group of students, who were considered "at-risk" because of poor grades and unstable home situations, consistently stated that they enjoyed visiting their "adopted" grandparents because it made them feel "like part of a family."

The success of the program spread by word of mouth and soon other principals began to inquire about it in hopes of starting their own program. Because a large number of schools displayed strong interest in initiating an AGP, the task of coordinating this endeavor was delegated to the DCPS's Department of Community Participation (DCP). Since the coordination quickly involved many hours to deal with such issues as "adoption" ceremonies, transportation needs, outings, etc., it was decided that the AGP should be evaluated to determine if the time personnel spent on the program justified the costs.

Consequently, staff from DCPS's Office of Education Accountability (OEA) were assigned to evaluate the program ·by using a quasi-experimental study involving a designated number of students and elderly participants. After deciding what variables to examine, OEA personnel created a quasi-experimental pre-test/post-test control group design to determine the program's impact on the students and on the elderly participants. The study would assess the effects on students' sense of self-esteem, and their attitudes toward the elderly as well as the program's effect on the elderly's level of depression, general self-esteem, and attitudes toward young children. These particular variables were chosen because a review of the research literature suggested that this type of intergenerational contact might have influence upon them (Brickell, 1979; Rosenthal, 1971; Snyder-Swann, 1978; Zung, 1967).

A statistical analysis of the quantitative data collected in the study suggested that AGP had a positive influence on pupils' perceptions of self-esteem, and considerably improved their attitudes toward the elderly (Proller, 1985) (see Table I). It did not, however, reduce depression levels of the elderly, increase their self-esteem or significantly alter their negative stereotypes about young children (Proller, 1986) (see Table II). Following a modification of the program, later data showed that the elderly's self-esteem increased, their depression levels decreased, and their negative attitudes toward youngsters were generally eliminated after about one school year of weekly intergenerational contact (Proller & Sanjurjo, 1987) (see Table III).

Since OEA's study indicated that AGP was having a positive effect upon both the children and the elderly, the AGP was continued and provided with additional funding.

At the present time, DCPS's AGP operates in over 50 elementary, middle and senior high schools in conjunction with about 50

TABLE I. Observed Variables — Children — 1985

Variance	Problem Children		Regular Children		Control Group	
	X	SD	X	SD	X	SD
CATE pre-test	85.58	8.69	88.27	21.97	76.50	10.86
CATE post-test	91.08	9.94	90.82	9.00	74.10	9.51
Piers-Harris pre-test	57.30	13.84	58.30	10.70	59.10	12.79
Piers-Harris post-test	63.77	11.88	65.61	10.69	60.55	13.15

TABLE II. Observed Variables — Elderly — 1985

Variable	Experimental Group		Control Group	
	$\bar{X}$ n = 32	SD	$\bar{X}$ n = 29	SD
EPATCH pre-test	62.70	17.09	63.95	16.91
EPATCH post-test	62.00	23.00	65.62	11.66
Beck Depression pre-test	11.30	10.21	11.43	11.72
Beck Depression post-test	7.40	8.67	8.57	8.57
Rosenberg Self-esteem pre-test	3.40	2.62	3.00	2.17
Rosenberg Self-esteem post-test	2.65	2.35	3.19	2.17

TABLE III. Observed Variables—Elderly—1987

Variable	Experimental Group		Control Group	
	X̄	SD	X̄	SD
	n = 28		n = 26	
EPATCH pre-test	61.30	16.98	62.95	16.73
EPATCH post-test	71.49	16.48	65.15	14.38
Beck Depression pre-test	10.89	9.88	11.12	10.73
Beck Depression post-test	3.13	7.64	8.59	9.38
Rosenberg Self-esteem pre-test	3.89	2.52	3.11	2.47
Rosenberg Self-esteem post-test	1.43	2.12	3.08	2.74

kinds of elderly facilities as well as various types of residential care facilities. It serves approximately 2,000 students and about 1,200 senior citizens.

The existing AGPs are as varied as the types of students and elderly facilities involved. Some serve only "at-risk" pupils while others deal only with gifted children, emotionally disturbed pupils, learning disabled youngsters, etc. As mentioned, the types of senior citizen facilities include elderly people who live at home but attend adult day care centers, senior citizens who live in adult congregate living facilities, and individuals who live in three different levels of residential care facilities. The summary of the data from a quasi-experimental study conducted by the OEA's evaluations of the DCPS Adoptive Grandparent program follows.

OVERVIEW

Method

Elementary-aged children visited nursing home residents on a regular basis for a period of four months. During the visits, the youngsters and the elderly interacted either on a one-to-one or group basis. The nature of the interactions was determined by the purpose of the particular visit. For example, if the pupils came during non-holiday times, they visited with a specific individual whom they had chosen as their "adopted grandparent." Youngsters and the elderly were matched on the basis of mutual interests. If the children came during a holiday time (like Christmas) the two groups would interact as one whole unit rather than on an individualized basis.

Subjects

The study involved a group of 13 volunteer 5th and 6th graders, identified by their teachers and counselors as "problem" children (i.e., the youngsters evidenced behavior problems at school and/or were the offspring of parents experiencing numerous financial and/ or emotional difficulties) and a group of 23 "regular" 5th and 6th grade pupils who also agreed to "adopt" grandparents who were living in a nearby public nursing home.

Since earlier research indicated that many at-risk students live in unstable home situations and as a result experience rejection and low self-esteem, the study decided to include a group of at-risk and "regular" youth in the initial study. The 23 "regulars" were students at the same grade level in the same school. The school was selected because of the principal's interest and the availability of funds to support transportation.

The elderly residents (all of whom were at least 60 years of age) voluntarily agreed to participate in the program. Matched control groups for the two groups of children as well as for the institutionalized elderly were utilized in this study. The control group of children attended a school with approximately the same demographic characteristics as the school involving the experimental subjects while the control group residents lived at a facility which provided the same level of care for its patients as the experimental facility. All the subjects, children as well as elderly, involved in this study represented the tri-ethnic population of Dade County (Hispanic, Haitian, Anglo).

Procedure

Prior to any contact between the children and the elderly, all experimental and control group youngsters completed two paper and pencil instruments, the *CATE*, which measures Children's Attitudes Toward the Elderly and the *Piers Harris Self-Esteem Scale*. The elderly experimental and control group subjects completed the *EPATCH*, which measures the Elderly's Perceptions about Children, the *Beck Depression Scale*, and the *Rosenberg Self-Esteem Scale*. Prior to meetings between the two groups of experimental subjects, nursing home staff, in conjunction with the youngsters' teachers, provided the students with an orientation regarding the purpose of a nursing home and the kinds of problems the facility's residents might be experiencing.

Design

The experimental design employed was a quasi-experimental pre-test, post-test matched control group design. The independent variable was the systematic contact between the children and the nursing home residents while the dependent variables for the children included attitudes toward the elderly and self-esteem. Dependent variables for the elderly were attitudes toward children, depression, and self-esteem.

Results

Statistical analyses of the data revealed the following results. Initially, an analysis of co-variance procedure was used to compare post-test differences between the institutionalized elderly experimental and institutionalized elderly control groups and the children's experimental and control groups on the various dependent variables. T-tests were performed within each group for all dependent variables to determine if any pre- and post-test differences appeared on any of them.

Controlling for any pre-test differences between the two elderly groups, the co-variance analysis showed no significant differences between the experimental group and the control group on any of the three instruments (i.e., the *EPATCH*, the *Beck Depression Scale*, and the *Rosenberg Self-Esteem Scale*. Furthermore, T-tests to ascertain the extent of within-group differences on the three instruments (for both the experimental and control group) also yielded similar results (see Table I).

The co-variance procedure utilized with the children's group revealed significant post-test differences on the *CATE* between both the two experimental groups (i.e., the "troubled" children and the "regular" children) and the control group, [F(2.48) = 14.85, p.05]. The paired T-test procedure employed to examine pre- and post-test differences within each group showed that for the "troubled" children, their attitudes toward the elderly improved and reached statistical significance (t = 2.0, p < .05). However, the "regular" children's attitudes toward the elderly and the control group children's attitudes toward the elderly showed little change and failed to meet either statistical or practical significance.

The ancova analysis of data collected on the *Piers Harris* revealed no significant post-test differences between the two experimental groups and the control group. The paired T-test analysis of the two experimental groups (i.e., the "troubled" children and the "regular" children) on the self-esteem instrument revealed significant differences between pre- and post-test scores for both groups (t = 2.57, p.02 and t = 3.29, p.00, respectively). The control group children had no statistical differences between their pre- and post-test scores (see Table II).

CONCLUSION

This study examined the effects of regular, systematic contact between institutionalized elderly and elementary school-aged children. It had in particular to ascertain the extent to which the frail elderly, who interact with elementary school children, might change their negative attitudes about children, decrease their depression levels, and increase their self-esteem as a function of interacting with children.

Initially, no significant changes were found in these variables. However, with program modification studies later revealed that the elderly's negative attitude were reversed, depression levels were decreased, and their self-esteem was increased. This data was reported when children increased their contact from monthly to weekly visits for an entire school year (Proller, 1986) (see Table III).

The results of analyzing quantitative data gathered from the children's groups suggested that even with limited amount of contact, both the control and experimental groups developed significantly improved attitudes toward the elderly. Though neither of the children's groups improved with regard to self-esteem in the early testing, after program modification later studies showed the "at-risk youngsters"' self-esteem did, indeed, improve significantly (Proller & Sanjurjo, 1987).

Additional research is currently being conducted with the AGP participants. Other variables being examined include AGP's impact on children's death anxiety, and moral development and its influence on elderly individuals' satisfaction, death anxiety, and Activities for Daily Living (ADL) skills.

DCPS is extremely proud of its AGP and it projects that it will eventually include over 200 schools and 200 facilities that are residents for the elderly.

REFERENCES

Altman, H.A. & Scollon, J. (1973). The influence of process variables on self-esteem. *Psychology, 10,* 37-43.

Brickell, C.M. (1979). Art bridges the age gap. *Innovation, 7,* University of Michigan School of Education. Ann Arbor: Michigan.

Mussen, P.H., Conger, J.J., & Kagan, J.A. (1969). *Child development and personality.* New York: Harper & Row.

Perky, W.W. (1970). *Self-concept and school achievement.* Englewood Cliffs: Prentice-Hall.

Proller, N. (1985, April). *The effects of systematic intergenerational contact between elementary-aged children and the frail elderly.* Paper presented at the meeting of the American Education Research Association, San Francisco, California.

Proller, N. & Sanjurjo, S. (1987, April). *Longitudinal outcomes of systematic intergenerational contact between elementary-aged children and the elderly.* Paper presented at the meeting of the American Education Research Association, Washington, DC.

Rosenberg, M. (1965). *Society and the adolescent self-image.* Princeton: Princeton University Press.

Rosenthal, R.C. (1971). Pygmalion reaffirmed. In J. Elashoff & R. Snow (Eds.), *Pygmalian reconsidered* (pp. 139-155). Worthington, Ohio: C.A. Jones.

Snyder, M. & Swann, W. (1978). Behavioral confirmation in social interaction. From social perception to social psychology. *Journal of Experimental Social Psychology, 14,* 148-162.

Zung, W.W.K. (1967). Depression in the normal aged. *Psychosomatics, 8,* 287-292.

Research Evaluation
of a Foster Grandparent Program

Rosalyn Saltz, PhD

SUMMARY. This paper describes the results of a longitudinal research paper evaluating the effect of a Foster Grandparent Program (FGP) on the personal development of its participants. It focuses on the hypotheses, methodology and outcome of a series of studies conducted at the Detroit Foster Grandparent Program, particularly as they relate to effects on the older participants.

Carefully executed evaluation research can be critical for future funding of social programs. For example, during the 1970s the future of continued federal funding for the United States Foster Grandparent Program (FGP) was in precarious balance. At that time, a number of federal administrators informed the writer that the United States FGP would probably not have survived, much less expanded to its present size, if intensive longitudinal research on one of its early pilot projects had not clearly demonstrated its beneficial effects on both older persons and on the children they helped.

To assess the effects of an intervention procedure on human development, researchers agree that the most definitive findings come from longitudinal studies which are based on experimental methods. In evaluating the effects of intergenerational programs on the personal development of their participants, for example, such methods would involve repeated comparisons over time of those who have participated in an intergenerational program with a carefully matched control group who have not. However, such strategies are often difficult and expensive to employ. Consequently, they have

Rosalyn Saltz is Professor of Education, University of Michigan-Dearborn, Child Development Center, Dearborn, MI 48128-1491.

been utilized infrequently in evaluation studies of intergenerational programs. One example of a longitudinal effect was a series of studies which evaluated the effects of a Detroit area Foster Grandparent Program on the personal development of its participants.

The United States Foster Grandparent Program, a federally sponsored intergenerational program initiated in 1965, aims to "combine the participation of older Americans who have love to give, and children with special needs who thrive on that love" (U.S. ACTION, 1980), currently administered by the federal agency ACTION. As of 1986 there were 262 Foster Grandparent projects in the United States and its territories with 26,600 foster grandparents serving more than 73,200 children in a wide variety of children's settings, including hospitals, youth homes, Head Start and day care centers, special needs classrooms, teen parent programs, and private homes (U.S. ACTION, 1987).

Now in its third decade, both the stated goals and specific functioning of the program has remained constant from its inception (U.S. ACTION, 1980). The conditions of older persons participation in the FGP, as well as their quasi-family role, are essentially the same in 1988 as they were in 1965. Foster grandparents must be a minimum of 60 years of age and with low incomes (as defined by federal guidelines). There are no educational requirements. They receive a small, non-taxable stipend, along with a daily meal, transportation, and some benefits. For 20 hours weekly, usually 5 days per week, their unique function is to provide "grandparenting" (i.e., individualized affection and attention to their 2 or 3 assigned foster grandchildren: as one foster grandparent put it, "To even spoil them like real grandparents do!"). The mutual nature of the program's goals for both its younger and older participants perhaps was captured best by another foster grandparent who stated simply, "I love him and he loves me. We help each other" (Saltz, 1985).

One of the first United States Foster Grandparent projects was implemented in a Detroit area institution for neglected and dependent children. In 1986, a group of 40 indigent older people, aged 60 to 75, became participants in the then fledgling Foster Grandparent Program. After 40 hours of pre-service training at the Merrill-Palmer institute of Detroit, the foster grandparents were assigned to the institution for 20 hours weekly to provide its young residents with "tender loving care."

The Detroit area project was the only one of the 20 Foster Grandparent pilot projects to be subjected to an independently funded, intensive evaluation. Over a period of seven years, a series of studies investigated the outcomes of the project on the personal development of its original participants, both children and foster grandparents. This research was conducted at the Merrill-Palmer Insititute, Wayne State University Institute of Gerontology, and the University of Michigan-Dearborn. Where possible, comparisons were made between findings for participants in the program and similar groups of non-participants ("Controls"). Issues relating to older persons as workers were also investigated. The results of a number of these studies have been reported previously (Saltz, 1969, 1971, 1973, 1985; Troll, Dunin-Marciewicz & Saltz, 1976; Dunin-Marciewicz, Troll & Saltz, 1982).

This paper will focus on the hypotheses, outcomes and methodology of the Detroit Foster Grandparent project studies, particularly as they relate to effects on the older participants. Especially since the goals and the operational details of the U.S. FGP have remained constant throughout its history, the findings of these studies may be of programmatic as well as scholarly and historical interest to those currently involved in similar intergenerational projects. The methodology of some of these studies will be described in some detail for those readers who may be interested in undertaking similar research.

THE DETROIT FOSTER GRANDPARENT PROGRAM AND THE CHILDREN

The site of the pioneer Detroit Foster Grandparent project was a progressive, attractive facility, located on a large wooded area of a Detroit suburb. It was operated by a Catholic religious order and was staffed by both nuns and laypersons. Its residents were neglected and dependent children from infancy to 12 years of age. If placed after early infancy, most resided in the institution for at least several years, some for all of their early childhoods and beyond.

Young children have been found to have intense needs for attachments to adults who can give them individualized affection and attention. Even benign and reasonably stimulating institutional atmospheres seem to constitute serious emotional deprivation for young children who typically experience developmental delays and social-emotional difficulties when reared in such environments (Yarrow, 1964). Prior to the introduction of the foster grandparents, the young children in the Detroit institution evidenced such developmental problems. By providing them with personalized, quasi-familial relationships, it was hoped that detrimental effects of their institutionalization would be minimized or reversed.

Each of the 40 foster grandparents was assigned two children under 6 years of age with whom they interacted five days per week, four hours per day. Usually, the children and their foster grandparents formed strong attachments, often in a surprisingly short period of time. Specific activities varied according to the children's ages and needs, but the mutually affective and family-like quality of the relationship were clear. A foster grandparent would refer to "my Johnny" or "my Sally" with great pride as she extolled her foster grandchild's virtues and accomplishments to any listener. Likewise, Johnny might tell another child, "I'm going to tell my grandpa!" and Sally would expectantly wait at the door for her "grandma" to arrive.

Effects on the children's social, verbal, and intellectual development were assessed for 81 children over a 4 year period, before and after they had experienced at least 4 months and up to 4 years of foster grandparenting in the institution. The control group was a comparable set of children in a very similar Baltimore institution where no foster grandparents were introduced. Assessment measures included standardized IQ and achievement tests, systematic observations, and periodic interviews with the children's caregivers and preschool teachers. The results indicated that foster grandparenting minimized greatly the detrimental effects that institutionalization can have on children's development, and it had clear, often dramatic positive impact on the children's social, verbal and intellectual development (for details, see Saltz, 1969, 1973).

THE FOSTER GRANDPARENTS

Questions and Hypotheses

What are the conditions conducive to the maintenance of life-satisfaction, vigor, and intellectual efficiency as people age? This is a major question of concern to those in the field of aging, and it was a minor focus of the Detroit study.

The hypotheses of the study in relation to outcomes for foster grandparents were that the regular, meaningful activity and affective social interactions involved in foster grandparenting would: (a) foster the life-satisfaction and self-esteem of the older people (b) positively affect their physical health and vigor, and (c) maintain their efficient intellectual functioning as measured by standard IQ tests.

These hypotheses were based on theory and research in the field of aging at the time of the initiation of the FGP, but they were far from self-evident. There was and is little dispute that poverty and poor health can interfere seriously with the life-satisfaction of older persons. More controversial has been the role of activity and social involvement in fostering their good life adjustment. There were many proponents of the "disengagement" theory (Cumming & Henry, 1961) which held that as people age, it is natural for them to gradually withdraw from previous activities and personal involvements, often with feelings of placid, detached contentment. This view has received less support over time (Sill, 1980), and it was countered by other gerontologists, like Birren (1964, p. 218), who maintained that "There are differences in the environments of older persons that affect their tendency to promote and maintain effective involvement and behavior which, in turn, increases their resistance to deteriorative attitudes and behaviors typified as senile."

Research evidence has been somewhat mixed on this issue of involvement and activity versus disengagement as correlates of life-satisfaction and deterioration. Several studies have indicated that those individuals who achieved life satisfaction with low activity levels prior to old age, continued this pattern into old age (Havighurst, Neugarten, & Tobin, 1968; Maddox, 1968). However, activity has been found to be more often associated with good life adjustment in older persons than is disengagement (Palmore, 1968). Most compelling, however, is that little contrary evidence has been offered to refute the fact that when disengagement is imposed by society against the individual's wishes, as Zborowski (1962, p. 309) stated, it can have "implications of isolation, frustration, bitterness, anxiety, illness, and eventually, death." As in the case of the FGP, most intergenerational programs are founded on the assumption that meaningful activity and social interactions will counter such negative consequences of enforced disengagement.

Secondary, but important, questions in the Detroit Foster Grandparent Project research studies were related to older persons as workers. The research questions and findings also addressed some of these issues.

METHODS

To evaluate the program's outcomes for the foster grandparents, assessments were made of their levels of life-satisfaction and adjustment, their intellectual efficiency, and their health status before, during, and after 7 years of their initial participation in the Detroit project. The results were compared with those of a group of controls. Assessment measures included an interview schedule (described further below), a standard IQ test, observations, health, attendance, longevity records, and supervisor ratings.

Sample

Fifty-nine older persons (37 foster grandparents and 22 controls) served as the subjects for the longitudinal studies. (Three of the original group of 40 foster grandparents left the program prior to completing their first year and were, therefore, dropped from the research sample.)

At the beginning of the project (1965), the foster grandparents in our sample were between 60 and 75 years of age, and were evenly divided between Blacks and Caucasians. Three were male and 34 were female. Only 20% had completed high school, and a fourth of the group had less than 9 years of formal education; 15% had some college. Two-thirds of the group had health ratings of good or excellent, while one-third were rated as being in only fair health.

The control group of older persons who did not participate in the FGP was selected so as to be as similar as possible to the foster grandparent sample. An analysis of the composition of the two groups on major demographic variables, including age, sex, race, education, and health, yielded only one statistically significant difference between them: number of grandchildren.

The Research Interview

Each research interview was administered individually, and involved many concrete visual aids and materials to make it appropriate and motivating for the older persons in the sample. The project's interview was adapted in part from other instruments reported in the literature.

The adapted subsections of the interview are: (a) *Ladder of Aspiration*, adapted from Cantril (1962). Here, the respondents first describe what would be the "best possible life" and the "worst possible life"; then, designate on a picture of a 10-stepped ladder where they feel they stand in the present, stood in the past, and will stand in the future; (b) *Total Adjustment Inventory*, a brief attitude inventory and a measure of morale, summed to produce a Total Adjustment score, adapted from Havighurst and Albrecht (1953) and Neugarten, Havighurst and Tobin (1961); and (c) *Semantic Differential Scale*, adapted from Osgood, Suei and Tannenbaum (1957). This scale lists pairs of adjectives such as "Weak-Strong," "Bad-Good," "Boring-Interesting" on a scale of one to seven, from positive to negative. The respondents choose the location on each scale for several concepts, such as "My friends think I am," "Young children," "Young people," and "Old people."

The interview also included a measure, "Five Questions." These call for free responses concerning possible beneficial or detrimental effects of the foster grandparent experience for both the children and for older people and for opinions on qualities needed for bringing up children. Responses were scored and analyzed according to a content coding system developed by project staff. The percentage of inter rater agreement on the coding categories was 92.2. (The complete Foster Grandparent Interview Schedule appears in Saltz, [1971], or is available from the writer.)

OUTCOMES FOR THE FOSTER GRANDPARENTS

Life-Satisfaction and Adjustment

Markedly positive effects on life-satisfaction and adjustment were found for the Detroit Foster Grandparents after 1 and 2 years of participation in the FGP, and again after 7 years. The foster grandparent experience appeared to meet the major requirements for life-satisfaction that the older persons had expressed in their pre-interviews. (This was determined by comparing the foster grandparents pre-post data from the "Five Questions" and "worst v. best life" Ladder of Aspiration measures described above, analyzed by repeated measure analysis of variance and t-tests.)

After 2 years in the program, the foster grandparents' responses on these measures showed a statistically significant increase in the overall level of their reported life-satisfaction and feelings of self-esteem. The major areas which they cited as contributing to their improved morale were the opportunity to engage in meaningful activity, feelings of purpose in life, improved financial situations, involvement in satisfying social contacts, and renewed feelings of independence, vigor, and usefulness. The feelings of renewed usefulness were almost always related directly to their important role as child caregivers, and their gratification that they were appreciated and loved by their foster grandchildren in return. "I am happier than in many years. I hope to say, in later years, I helped that boy!" and "I think it's a wonderful thing you're still wanted and needed" were typical responses during the foster grandparent interviews.

These positive changes were found again for the foster grandparents in the 7 year follow-up study where portions of the original interview were readministered to the original foster grandparents and the control group. Now ranging in age from 69 to 82, almost half of the original group of 40 foster grandparents were still actively involved in the program (Troll et al., 1973). The active foster grandparents maintained their high level of life satisfaction along the same dimensions described above. They were also more optimistic about the future than was a comparable national sample of older persons their age (Dunin, Narciewicz et al., 1982). Many of the positive effects, particularly those related to improved self-esteem, persisted also for those who had left the program (most for health reasons) prior to the follow-up study. As one former foster grandparent stated, "I'll always remember, I'll always know how much I helped that child. I didn't think I could do such a thing at my age!" These effects were most noticeable when the current and former foster grandparent group was compared with their controls, who had never participated in the program (Troll et al., 1973).

IQ Results

As an estimate of intellectual level and efficiency, four subtests of the Wechsler Adult Intelligence Scale (Wechsler, D., 1955) were administered to the 40 foster grandparents when they began their assignments at the Detroit institution in 1965, and again in 1972, to 28 of these individuals (18 still in the program and 10 who had dropped out). The four subtests were: Vocabulary, Similarities, Block Design, and Digit Span.

At the initiation of the project, the foster grandparents' estimated total WAIS IQs ranged from 81 (below average) to 122 (superior) with a mean of 102 (average). For the 28 foster grandparents in the post-test condition, the mean total pre-IQ was 96, while the mean post IQ was 104. This slight improvement was statistically significant.

Neither relative age of subjects on the first testing nor their IQ at that time predicted direction of change on retesting. The subjects who left the project during the 7 years were significantly lower in their initial IQ than those who remained.

Health, Longevity, and Work Performance of the Foster Grandparents

The results relating to foster grandparenting effects on the health of the participants are mixed. About half of the group after two years cited subjective feelings of health and vigor as a major benefit of foster grandparenting, as for example, "I feel better. I have no time for pains! or "Our health is much better than it would be if we were sitting around without anything to do or anyone to love!" Also, the foster grandparents' record of absence due to illness compared very favorably with a national sample of working people and even more favorably with a housekeeping sample in their age group (Saltz, 1971). On the other hand, after 2 years, 46% of the foster grandparents expressed some concern about health, at least for "some of those who can't take it," and declining health was cited as a reason for dropping out of the program by 13 of the 18 who were no longer in the program at the 7 year follow-up. In contrast to those who were still participating in the program, the terminated group did not include benefits to health as one of the advantages that had gained from foster grandparenting. On balance, however, while not a panacea, foster grandparenting appeared to have positive effects on the perceived health and vigor of many of the older people.

As workers, the foster grandparents proved to be dependable and increasingly valued by their supervisors as time went on. The factor most predictive of longevity and success as a foster grandparent was a statement in their initial interviews to the effect that they perceived their primary role as foster grandparents as that of giving the children love. Other factors related to foster grandparent success and longevity were relatively high IQ test results and positive life attitudes at the initial assessments. It is of interest that neither relative health status nor age at their entry to the program proved related to foster grandparent longevity.

CONCLUSIONS

The positive longitudinal research results on the effectiveness of the federal FGP concept have since been supported by other studies. They are also supported by the many subsequent successful implementations of federal Foster Grandparent Projects and other similar intergenerational programs which have extended the foster grandparent concept beyond its original applications (Saltz, 1985).

The history of the FGP and its Detroit area evaluation also is of interest from another perspective: it suggests the importance of applied research in the arena of public funding. The intensive, data based, and longitudinal nature of the Detroit studies and its positive findings provided an important support to those fighting for Congressional backing to maintain and extend the U.S. Foster Grandparent Program. This would suggest that careful, longitudinal studies of outcomes of intergenerational programs can further important social, as well as scholarly goals. It is hoped that many more such studies of current developments in the field will be undertaken and will receive the support they need to be successfully completed.

REFERENCES

Cantril, H., & Free, L.A. (1962, Oct). Hopes and fears for self and country: The self anchoring striving scale in cross-cultural research. *The American Behavioral Scientist*. Supplement, 6.

Cumming, E., & Henry, W.E. (1961). *Growing old: The process of disengagement*. New York: Basic Books.

Dunin-Marciewicz, A., Troll, L., & Saltz, R. (1982, March). *Life satisfaction of foster grandparents: Past, present, future*. Paper presented at meeting of Michigan Academy of Science, Arts and Letters, Kalamazoo, MI.

Havighurst, R.J., & Albrecht, R. (1953). Life satisfaction scales. *Older People*. Toronto: Longmans, Green & Co.

Havighurst, R.J., Neugarten, B.L., & Tobin, S. (1968). Disengagement and patterns of aging. In B.L. Neugarten (Ed.), *Middle age and aging*. Chicago: The University of Chicago Press, pp. 161-177.

Maddox, G.L. (1966). Persistence of life style among the elderly: A longitudinal study of patterns of social activity in relation to life satisfaction. In Neugarten, B.L. (Ed.), *Middle Age and Aging*. Chicago: The University of Chicago Press.

Neugarten, B., Havighurst, R.J., & Tobin, S. (1961). The measurement of life satisfaction. *Journal of Gerontology, 16*, 134-143.

Osgood, C.E., Suei, G., & Tannenbaum, C.S. (1957). *The measure of meaning*. Urbana: University of Illinois Press.

Palmore, E.B. (1968). The effects of aging on activities and attitudes. *Gerontologist, 8*, 256-263.

Saltz, R. (1969). Counteracting the effects of stress in young institutionalized children. In Rourke, B.P. (Ed.), *Explorations in the psychology of stress and anxiety*. Don Mills, Ont: Longmans, pp. 77-89.

Saltz, R. (1971). Aging persons as child-care workers in a foster grandparent program: Psychosocial effects and work performance. *Aging and Human Development, 23*, 314-340.

Saltz, R. (1973). Effects of part-time mothering on IQ and SQ of young children. *Child Development, 44*, 166-170.

Saltz, R. (1985). "We help each other:" The U.S. Foster Grandparent Program. In K. Struntz & S. Reville (Eds.), *Growing together: An international source-*

book. Washington, DC: American Association for Retired Persons. Palm Springs, CA: Elvirita Lewis Foundation.

Sill, J.S. (1980). Disengagement reconsidered: Awareness of finitude. *Gerontologist, 20*, 456-462.

Troll, L., Saltz, R., & Dunn-Marciewicz, A. (1973). *A seven year followup of a foster grandparent group*. Paper presented at meeting of Gerontological Society, Miami Beach, FL.

Troll, L. (1976). A seven-year follow-up of a group of foster grandparents. *Journal of Gerontology, 31* (5), 583-585.

U.S. ACTION (1980). *Foster grandparent program: 15 years serving children with special needs: A touch of love*. Washington, DC: Action Pamphlet No. 44006.

U.S. ACTION (1987). *ACTION news fact sheet: Foster grandparent program*, Washington, DC: Mimeo.

Wechsler, D. (1955). *Wechsler adult intelligence scale*, New York: Psychological Corporation.

Yarrow, L.J. (1964). Separation from parents during early childhood. In M.L. Hoffman & L. Hoffman (Eds.), *Review of child development research*. New York: Russel Sage Foundation, pp. 89-136.

Intergenerational Program Research to Refine Theory and Practice

Donald Cohon, PhD

SUMMARY. This paper briefly reviews a number of theories that provide the rationale for undertaking intergenerational programs and upon which intergenerational research concepts are based. After discussing the importance of using these theories to establish the framework within which program research occurs, a number of recent studies are reviewed and implications for future research and practice are presented.

In the past two decades the potential benefits of intergenerational programs to individuals, families, and society have increasingly been recognized (McCaslin, 1983; Saltz, 1970; Saltz, 1971; Struntz & Reville, 1985). As numbers of these programs have grown, there have been parallel efforts to assess their effects on both elderly and young participants. In contrast to evaluation which is an integral part of program management and development, research efforts are intended to support or disprove general theories and principles. A general description of appropriate research methodology has been reviewed elsewhere (Birren & Cunningham, 1985; Cohon, 1985). This paper briefly describes a number of theories that provide the rationale for undertaking intergenerational programs and from which the concepts studied with intergenerational research are drawn. It also describes findings from selected studies and discusses the implications for future research.

Donald Cohon is Director, ICARE, Box 262, Star Route, Muir Beach, CA 94965.

IDEOLOGICAL CONSIDERATIONS

Before describing theoretical frameworks, a practical issue is important to consider. The political arena is one context within which intergenerational research has an effect because it may be used to provide support for or against the "intergenerational inequity" debate that has gained prominence during the present Federal Administration. This ideological issue has emerged in response to declining budgets for government programs. Intergenerational inequity frames policy issues in terms of competition and conflict between young and old over the distribution of diminishing resources (Kingson, Hirshorn & Harootyan, 1987). In contrast to this position is the notion of the "interdependence of generations" which draws on traditional theories of human development to advocate that different generations are mutually dependent and are continually involved in transferring services, finances, knowledge and technology, culture, and various governmental benefits between one another (Kingson et al., 1987). In light of this controversy, research findings from studies of intergenerational programs have immediate practical implications for policy decisions and program support.

THEORETICAL FOUNDATIONS

Outside of the political arena, the interdependence of generations' position has its roots in human life cycle and cultural preservation theories. Erikson (1982) posits the final two stages of human development as generativity, defined as primarily the concern for establishing and guiding the next generation and ego integrity, the acceptance of one's one and only life cycle as appropriate and meaningful. Similarly, Mannheim and Stewart (1962) are concerned with the transmission of the "basic inventory of group life" or cultural traditions for the adequate functioning of the individual as well as for the continuance of society. Butler and Lewis (1973) draw a parallel conclusion about "special characteristics" of older people: (a) desire to leave a "legacy" — something of themselves behind after they died (legacy provides a sense of continuity, giving the older person a feeling of being able to participate even after death), and (b) closely connected with "legacy" is a natural propensity of the old to share with the young the accumulated knowledge and experiences they have collected. Butler (1968) calls this universal occurrence the "life review."

A number of theories attempt to describe a universal aging process. After reviewing some of the seminal theories on aging, for example the multiple stress model (Lowenthal, 1967), the disengagement theory (Cumming & Henry, 1961), activity theory (Lemon, Bengston & Petersen, 1972), and social breakdown syndrome (Kuypers & Bengston, 1973) what emerges is a recognition that it is quite unlikely that uniform aging processes can be identified and consequently many different paradigms for age changes and behavior must be considered. Baltes and Labouive (1973) argue that the search for a universal aging process follows an erroneous "stability" model, and they assert that aging phenomenon will be highly labile and subject to dramatic modifications as a reflection of rapidly changing environmental and biological contexts. Lawton and Nahemow (1973) have sketched an ecological theory of adaptive behavior of aging in which the aging process is one of continual adaptation to external environmental demands and to the changes in internal capabilities and functioning which take place over the life cycle.

In the past decade, more attention has been paid by researchers to articulating the relationship between these theories and the variables or concepts that are derived from them. Mangen and Petersen (1982) provide a comprehensive review of research instruments used in social gerontology containing chapters devoted to concepts frequently used in intergenerational research studies: Morale and Life Satisfaction (Saurer & Warland, 1982); Self-Concept and Self-Esteem (Breytspraak & George, 1982; Bengston, Reedy & Gordon, 1985) and Perceptions of Old People (McTavish, 1982). McCaslin (1983) writing about the benefits of volunteerism to older workers' overall well-being (especially their mental health, morale, and life satisfaction) uses Friedman and Havighurst's analysis of the meanings and functions of work as the framework within which to examine a number of studies of many of these same variables. George and Bearon (1980) divide the concept of quality of life into two subjective dimensions, life satisfaction and self-esteem, and two objective dimensions, general health/functional status and socio-economic status.

In summary, a number of life span developmental theories and theories of aging form the foundation for a number of research variables used in intergenerational studies, and these include: self-concept, self-esteem, self-respect, well-being, morale, life satisfaction, physical health, mental health, economic factors, meaningful role relationships, meaningful life experiences, social contacts, and cognitive functioning.

In addition to theories of aging, child development theories also provide conceptual support for undertaking intergenerational research. Some theorists have viewed the shift from an agrarian to an industrial economy as the major factor contributing to the breakdown of the extended family network, increased ageism and age segregation, societal normlessness, individual personality disorders, and suicide (Durkheim, 1897/1951; Mead, 1960). Demographic patterns over the past 30 years reflect a movement away from three generation nuclear families (Havighurst, 1973) and recently show increases in single parent families and higher rates of divorce. Developmental theorists generally agree that infants and children need stable, consistent, adult role models for optimum psycho-social and cognitive development (Bronfenbrenner, 1967; Kohlberg, 1964). Others have suggested that isolation of the elderly is based, in part, on younger generations' negative perceptions of the elderly (Jantz et al., 1976). In summary, these theories offer support for the position that programs providing opportunities for increased contact and interaction between young children and the elderly should contribute to the child's overall learning (both socio-affective and cognitive), reduce negative attitudes of both groups toward each other, and influence later moral and personal development of the maturing child.

SELECTED STUDIES

Saltz (1985) summarizes results of studies of the Foster Grandparent Program conducted over a seven-year period. These studies are examples of longitudinal quasi-experimental applied research with a pre-test design using matched samples for both elderly and children. It is noteworthy that the matched sample groups of elderly are people with "active life styles." She presents a succinct analysis of several theoretical positions as well as Havighurst's (1969) critique of these attempts to describe a universal aging process

(Saltz, 1970; Saltz, 1971). Her work sets a standard for intergenerational research since it is grounded in theory and uses established psychometric instruments and principles of implementation. Variables for the elderly, derived from theories she discusses, include life adjustment, morale, and life satisfaction (these scales were combined to form a total adjustment score), and self-concept. Not only did statistical analyses of pre- and post-measures show significant increases for purposeful activity, financial status, health, social relationships, and living arrangements, but also content analysis of responses add a qualitative dimension to the findings. To the question, "What is the best possible life for you?" typical responses focused on the ability to continue working such as "happy . . . as long as I am able to do the job I am doing now" (Saltz, 1971, p. 325). A follow-up study showed that benefits to the elderly participants persisted for seven years or more after the initial assessments were completed. Another finding important for recruitment and selection was the predictive power for elderly participants' success in the foster grandparent role of their initial attitudes that children needed love in order to thrive and that their primary role in the Foster Grandparent Program was to offer the children affection.

Saltz' (1970) research on the effects of the Foster Grandparent Program on young institutionalized children also uses a matched sample and studies the variables of cognitive and socio-emotional development. These concepts were selected after Saltz reviewed theories of a number of developmental psychologists noting the importance of early experience to later intellectual and social competence and the detrimental effects of institutionalization on children. Cognitive development was measured with the Cattel Infant Intelligence Test of Children under 30 months and the Stanford-Binet Intelligence Scale, Form LM, 3rd revision for those 30 months and over. Socio-emotional development was assessed with the Vineland Scale of Social Maturity. The latter was completed by the supervisor in charge of each child's cottage. Saltz (1970) interprets the results as follows. ". . . that for young children some form of relatively long-term, consistent quasi-family relationship with a single adult is conducive to fully adequate intellectual and social development" (p. 82), and she concludes that foster grandparenting had a positive impact in these areas (Saltz, 1985).

Newman, Vasudev and Onawola (1985) investigated elderly participants' perceptions of the effects of a school volunteer experience. Their dependent variable was psychological well-being derived from theories of aging that propound disengagement of activity as the "normal" course of life cycle. The authors present a brief discussion of these positions as a rationale for involving older persons in school volunteer programs. The research approach used primarily qualitative data and is descriptive in nature. The authors acknowledge limitations in their methodology. One hundred and eighty older volunteers, half of whom were male and half female, with a mean age of 64.4 from varied educational backgrounds (although 55% had some college education) were selected in equal numbers from three school volunteer programs in New York, Los Angeles, and Pittsburgh. The length of their volunteer experience ranged from three months to more than five years. Instrumentation consisted of the Questionnaire for School Volunteers (QSV) and the Interview Protocol for School Volunteers (IPSV) both constructed especially for use in this study. No formal validation procedures were conducted, and the authors recognize this as another limitation to this study. Despite these limitations, the statements of the seniors add more information to the growing body of data supporting the position that school volunteer experience does affect psychological well-being by giving meaningful structure to the lives of the participating elderly, providing a sense of being needed, and offering and enriching experience as well as enhancing self-esteem and coping skills.

Another approach to intergenerational research draws upon the works of Butler (1968), Myerhoff (1980) and Sherman (1985) by combining life history-taking with quantitative psychometric measurement. Using young people to conduct life-history interviews, the Brookdale Center on Aging carried out the Intergenerational Life History Project (see Disch & Moody, this edition). Although more than 200 people participated in the project in 1985, pre- and post-survey data is available for only 17 elderly and 45 young persons about whom little descriptive information is known. The rationale for involving young persons in this life review experience is explained by Strimling (1986), who asserts that the intergenerational interaction becomes ". . . the process of cultural transmission, a process that has broken down in our world of transient culture, transient morality, transient skills, and segregated generations'' (p. 8). The primary hypothesis of the study was that both groups would show improved self-esteem and have greater understanding and more positive attitudes toward one another. In addition, elderly participants were expected to have increased trust in younger persons and to show improved morale. Assessment instruments included the Bradburn Affect-Balance Scale (Bradburn, 1969); Rosenberg Self-Esteem Scale (Rosenberg, 1965); a six item Trust in Young People Scale and a general Reaction Survey with ten items focusing on attitudinal, cognitive and behavioral changes attributed to the program.

Both the Bradburn and Rosenberg Scales have been used successfully with older populations, although Mangen (1982) strongly recommends further reliability and validity assessment of the Bradburn. No reliability or validity measures of the other two instruments were conducted. Both the young and elderly participants completed the Rosenberg Scale and the General Reaction Survey while the elderly also completed the other two instruments. Findings indicated that both the elderly and the young had improved self-concepts, although there were inconsistencies in the elders' responses as well as in their responses to the Affect Balance Scale. The author raises questions about the elderly's ability to independently complete the various surveys, a factor which may have influenced the outcome. Not surprisingly, after the interview contacts, elders' trust in youth increased. Both groups had very positive evaluations of their overall participation in the program, and the author concluded that the project did ''enrich the lives of the participants'' (Disch, 1985).

Some social scientists attribute age segregation and social isolation of the elderly to younger persons' negative perceptions of aging. Taking note that the existing research findings of children's attitudes toward the elderly are inconsistent, Marks, Newman and Onawola (1985) developed the Children's Views on Aging questionnaire (CVoA) to give a more differentiated view of the individual components that make up latency-aged (8-10-year-old) children's attitudes toward aging. This is an important step in refining the construct ''attitude'' which is acknowledged by researchers to be a complex, labile variable. There were two major questions to the research: ''(a) What are the cognitive (descriptive), affective (evaluative), and conative (intentional) contents of children's attitudes toward the elderly, and (b) How do children's attitudes toward the elderly differ from their attitudes toward young people?'' (p. 91). This research design is an example of a cross-sectional survey to collect data at one point in time from a sample selected for its heterogeneity in order to generalize to a larger population of children. Four public schools in rural and urban locations in Western Pennsylvania provided 256 latency-aged children from grades three, four and five. The children were male and female and ethnically mixed, both black and white. The CVoA is a 53 item instrument with open-ended and closed-ended questions in a semantic differential scale.

The authors state that the CVoA ''measures the cognitive, affective, and conative aspects of children's attitudes'' (p. 92) with cognitive representing knowledge; affective, the feelings and subjective evaluations; and conative, the intended actions about the attitude object. The CVoA was validated for concurrent validity. Test re-test reliability and internal consistency were performed for the semantic differential, and the responses to the open-ended portion were compared with the corresponding questions to the semantic differential. The instrument was administered orally to the students by the first author during the normal school day with the introductory comment that this was not a test but rather questions to find out ''what you think.'' Data were analyzed using both descriptive and inferential statistics. Findings reaffirm that children's attitudes are not unidimensional (that is, either good or bad), and when responding to questions about the elderly, children consciously or unconsciously evaluate each attitude dimension separately with some being positive and some negative. Generally, the children had positive attitudes toward elders and they indicated positive behavioral intentions with response to open-ended questions suggesting a clear desire to interact with elderly in their classrooms. The authors conclude that this latter finding has important implication for using the elderly as classroom resources.

One weakness in using new psychometric instruments is the absence of repeated use with other populations and consistent reliability and validity findings. Hanusa and Newman (1988) in a recent technical report begin to address this point by focusing on 1987 studies using a revised version of the CVoA and examining test re-test reliability of the instrument as well as concurrent validity of the CVoA and the Children's Attitudes Toward the Elderly (Seefeldt et al., 1977). The first reliability study was conducted at one school just north of Pittsburgh that has been involved with intergenerational programs and has senior volunteers in most classrooms. Thirty-seven students, 19 males and 18 females, participated in completing the CVoA twice within a two-week time period. Summary measures of consistency developed because the open-ended format showed approximately 65% agreement over time which is acceptable for such an instrument, but suggest the need for further refinement and replications of the CVoA with other populations. The concurrent validity portion of this analysis was not available for review at this time.

DISCUSSION

It is apparent from the examples of intergenerational research reviewed that weaknesses continue to be found with both psychometric technology and the theoretical grounding of variables chosen for study. Saltz' work is an exception. In Disch's study only the Rosenberg Self-Esteem Scale has available research evidence supporting its use with older populations (Breytspraak & George, 1982). Marks, Newman and Onawola (1985) acknowledge the limitations of their instruments and indicate that the research is qualitative and descriptive. Although the authors indicate that they are studying "the impacts of volunteering on psychological well-being" (p. 123), they cite only one definition of this construct and make no comparative analyses of it in light of other theories. Only the evaluation portion of Disch's work was available to review for this paper, and it contained no theoretical explanation for the choice of variables to be analyzed nor did it relate findings to a theoretical position. Future intergenerational research analysis of data drawn from psychological measurement instruments would benefit from more explicit formulation of dependent variables and discussion of the findings in terms of specific theories.

Several other issues warrant further comment. The present climate of fiscal conservatism has not only given rise to the intergenerational inequity debate but also influences the goals and methodology of research. Proponents of intergenerational programs feel a need to bolster their position and to make an impact with their findings for policy and fiscal purposes. While influencing policy and fiscal decisions is a recognized goal of program evaluation (Anderson & Ball, 1978), it is the least technically developed and departs from the research ideal of objective assessment of program effects to test hypotheses and refine theories. Pragmatists would point out that reality necessitates such an effort, but, if this is to be the case, then it should be explicated. While there is an intuitive appeal for intergenerational programs, the need to support this view with scientific findings, that is with "hard". (i.e., quantitative) data, dictates selection of a research methodology that yields such data. But control groups are used only infrequently and inconsistencies often appear in the data that is produced.

Intergenerational researchers can use previous findings to assist with practical programmatic decisions and at the same time further test theoretical propositions. Existing research has already demonstrated that elderly with an activity orientation and with views that children need love and affection are more likely to be successful participants in intergenerational programs (Saltz, 1971; Newman et al., 1985). Since activity theorists postulate that persons are predisposed to maintain lifelong habits, commitments and preferences, research designs can test this hypothesis by recruiting both active and inactive elderly for intergenerational programs and examining differences between them and with matched control groups. The choice of what variables to examine is informed by the particular aspects of the theories and might include morale or life satisfaction, self-concept or self-esteem, etc. Such research on activity types may lead to the development of ancillary hypotheses that can be explored using the case study approach. For example, the identification of lifelong values and themes that give meaning to one's activity and may also function to maintain role and identify continuity in late life (Kaufman, 1986).

Social Breakdown Syndrome (SBS) Theory suggests other hypotheses that are testable through intergenerational research. Kuypers and Bengtson (1973) argue that allowing more self-determination for the elderly by meaningfully involving them in defining their own roles in late life is an intervention in the vicious feedback loop with negative inputs that characterizes SBS. These authors view programs of volunteerism as potential forms of tokenism unless the elderly are included in decision making from the outset. This proposition can be tested by designing research that involves one group of elderly early in the planning and seeks their input throughout the implementation of an intergenerational program and compares them with a matched sample that is not involved in planning or implementation.

As demonstrated by Newman, Marks and Onawola (1985), people are complex and have multiple, sometimes conflicted responses at different levels of awareness to interpersonal relationships. Quantitative analysis of data from measurement instruments does provide clues and give direction for further inquiry, but there is a procrustean character to statistical manipulation. Although qualitative research is sometimes described as "soft," a negative connotation, this type of data conveys a richness, a humanism that a purely empirical science denies (Sacks, 1983). Technically sound psychometric principles and methods should be complemented with clinical examples and detailed case studies. For example, using an anthropologist to observe in settings before starting an intergenerational program can provide valuable contextual information and perhaps detect subtle shifts in an environment that participants themselves may be unaware of. To paraphrase Neugarten (1973), there is a need to document different patterns of behavior with different types of elderly in different contexts with different types of children. In keeping with ecological theories of aging, such knowledge would be helpful in achieving a better fit or match between certain groups of elderly and particular activities including intergenerational ones.

In conclusion, intergenerational program research should aim to refine relevant theories in a manner that contributes to practical aspects of program development. It should not be limited to quantitative methodology but utilize an integrative approach that combines clinical and case study information with statistical findings.

BIBLIOGRAPHY

Anderson, S.B. & Ball, S. (1978). *The profession and practice of program evaluation*. San Francisco: Jossey Bass.
Baltes, P.B. & Labouive, T.V. (1973). Adult development of intellectual performance: Descriptive explanation and modification. In C. Eisdorfer & M.P.

Lawton (Eds.), *The psychology of adult development and aging*. Washington, DC: American Psychological Association.

Bengston, V.L., Reedy, M.N., & Gordon, C. (1985). Aging and self-conceptions: Personality processes and social contexts. In J. E. Birren & K.W. Schaie (Eds.), *Handbook of the psychology of aging* (2nd ed., pp. 544-585). New York: Van Nostrand Reinhold.

Birren, J.E. & Cunningham, W. (1985). Research on the psychology of aging: Principles, concepts and theory. In J.E. Biren & K.W. Schaie (Eds.), *Handbook of the psychology of aging* (2nd ed., pp. 23-30). New York: Van Nostrand Reinhold.

Bradburn, N.M. (1969). *The structure of psychological well being*. Chicago: University of Chicago Press.

Breytspraak, L.M. & George, L.K. (1982). Self-concept & self-esteem. In D.J. Mangen & W.A. Peterson (Eds.), *Clinical and social psychology: Volume 1*. Minneapolis: University of Minnesota Press.

Bronfenbrenner, U. (1972). *Influence on human development*. New York: Dryden Press.

Butler, R.N.. & Lewis, M.I. (1973). *Aging and mental health: Positive psychological approaches*. Saint Louis: C.V. Mosby.

Butler, R.N. (1968). The life review: An interpretation of reminiscence the aged. In B.L. Neugarten (Ed.), *Middle age and aging*. Chicago: University of Chicago Press.

Cohon, J.D. (1985). *Survey research as the initial step in developing intergenerational projects*. (Occasional paper series no. 505). Palm Springs: The Elder Press.

Cummings, E. & Henry, W.E. (1961). *Growing old*. New York: Basic Books.

Disch, R. (1985). *The intergenerational oral life history project*. New York: Hunter College, Brookdale Center on Aging.

Durkheim, E. (1951). *Suicide – a study in sociology*. G. Simpson (Ed. and trans.) New York: The Free Press.

Erikson, E. (1982). *The life cycle completed*. New York: W.W. Norton.

George, L. & Bearon, L. (1980). *Quality of life in older persons: Meaning and measurement*. New York: Human Sciences Press.

Hanusa, B.H. & Newman, S. (1988, February). *Technical report on the reliability of the children's views on aging (CVoA) scale*. Unpublished manuscript. (Available from Generations Together, 811 William Pitt Union, University of Pittsburgh, Pittsburgh, PA 15260)

Havighurst, R.J., Neugarten, B.L., & Tobin, S. (1973). Disengagement and patterns of aging. In B.L. Neugarten (Ed.), *Middle age and aging*. Chicago: University of Chicago Press.

Jantz, R.K., Seefeldt, C., Galper, A., & Serock, K. (1976). *Children's attitudes toward the elderly: Final report*. College Park: University of Maryland.

Kagan, J. & Moss, H.A. (1962). *Birth to maturity*. New York: Wiley.

Kaufman, S.R. (1986). *The ageless self-sources of meaning in late life*. Madison: University of Wisconsin Press.

Kingson, E., Hirshorn, B., & Harootyan, L. (1987). *The common stake: The interdependence of generations*. Washington, DC: Gerontological Society of America.

Kohlberg, S. (1964). Development of moral character and moral ideology. In M.L. Hoffman & L.W. Hoffman (Eds.), *Child development research: Volume 1*. New York: Russell Sage Foundation.

Kuypers, J.A. & Bengston, V.L. (1973). Social breakdown and competence: A model of normal study. *Human Development*, *16*(3), 181-202.

Lawton, M.P. & Nahemow, L. (1973). Ecology and the aging process. In C. Eisdorfer & M.P. Lawton (Eds.), *The psychology of adult development and aging*. Washington, DC: American Psychological Association.

Lemon, B.W., Bengtson, V.L., & Petersen, J.A. (1972). An exploration of the activity theory of aging: Activity types and life satisfaction among in-movers to a retirement community. *Journal of Gerontology*, *27*(4), 511-523.

Lowenthal, M.F. (1961). *Aging and mental disorder in San Francisco*. San Francisco: Jossey Bass.

Mangen, D.J. & Peterson, W.A. (Eds.). (1982). *Clinical and social psychology: Volume 1*. Minneapolis: University of Minnesota Press.

Mannheim, K. & Stewart, W.A. (1962). *An introduction to the sociology of education*. London: Routledge & Kegan.

Marks, R., Newman, S., & Onawola, R. (1985). Latency aged children's views of aging. *Educational Gerontology*, *11*(2/3), 89-99.

McCaslin, R. (1983). Current knowledge and questions regarding the use of older workers in mental health systems: The state of the art. In R. McCaslin (Ed.), *The older person as a mental health worker*. New York: Springer Publishing.

McTavish, D.G. (1982). Perceptions of old people. In D. Mangen & W. Peterson (Eds.), *Clinical and social psychology: Volume 1*. Minneapolis: University of Minnesota Press.

Mead, M. (1960). Culture change and character structure. In M. Stein, A. Vidich & D. White (Eds.), *Identity and anxiety*. New York: Free Press.

Neugarten, B.L. (1973). Personality change in late life: A developmental perspective. In C. Eisdorfer & M.P. Lawton (Eds.), *The psychology of adult development and aging*. Washington, DC: American Psychological Association.

Rosenberg, M. (1965). *Society and the adolescent self-image*. Princeton, NJ: Princeton University Press.

Sacks, O. (1983). *Awakenings* (rev. ed.). New York: E.P. Dutton.

Saltz, R. (1970). *Effects of a foster grandparent program on the intellectual and social development of young children in institutions*. Unpublished doctoral dissertation, Wayne State University, Detroit, MI.

Saltz, R. (1971). Aging persons as child-care workers in a foster grandparent program: Psycho-social effects and work performance. *Aging and Human Development*, *2*, 314-340.

Saltz, R. (1985). We help each other: The U.S. foster grandparents program. In K. Struntz & S. Reville (Eds.), *Growing together: An intergenerational sourcebook*. Washington, DC: American Association of Retired Persons; Palm Springs, CA: The Elvirita Lewis Foundation.

Sauer, W.J. & Warland, W. (1982). Morale and life satisfaction. In D. Mangen

& W. A. Peterson (Eds.), *Clinical and social psychology: Volume 1*. Minneapolis: University of Minnesota Press.

Seefeldt, C., Jantz, R.K., Galper, A., & Serock, K. (1977). Using pictures to explore children's attitudes toward the elderly. *The Gerontologist, 17*(6), 506-512.

Sherman, E. (1985). *Using reminiscence groups to enhance the social and emotional resources of community elderly*. Unpublished manuscript. (Available from Ringel Institute of Gerontology, School of Social Welfare, SUNY, Albany, NY 12222.)

Strimling, A. (1986, Winter). Doing talking: The storytelling relationship. *The Brookdale Center on Aging Newsletter, 8*(3).

PART IV:
TRENDS

Introduction

In the concluding articles, three authors present their views on the current and future need for intergenerational programs in relationship to their value of children, older persons and families.

Former Secretary of Health, Education and Welfare, Arthur S. Fleming, begins this Part IV with a statement on "Health Care: An Intergenerational Issue." He presents some of the nation's new health care efforts through the National Health Care Campaign and underscores the recognition that health care is an intergenerational issue.

In "A Case for Intergenerational Child Care," Ellen Galinsky examines the statistical need for child care, based on the increase in two working parent families, and reviews current efforts to address child care needs utilizing the skills and capacities of older people.

In "The Intergenerational Movement and its Relationship to Children and Families: An Interview with Margaret McFarland, PhD," McFarland states that the loss of the sharing of appropriate multi-generational responsibilities and functions in our society is one of the most important issues of our time. She points out that the move from supportive extended families to small isolated nuclear families has created many instabilities in modern life, and that intergenerational programs offer a real replacement for the loss of the supports of the extended family.

Sally Newman, PhD
Steven W. Brummel, MA

Health Care:
An Intergenerational Issue

Arthur S. Fleming, JD

After years of procrastination, our nation is giving serious consideration to doing something about the suffering caused by our patchwork health care system.

This is encouraging. But what is equally encouraging is a growing recognition that we cannot move forward in the area of health care unless we recognize that we are dealing with an intergenerational issue.

We know that there are 37 million persons in our nation under the age of 65 who are not under any kind of a health plan (public or private). We also know that 60 percent of this number are in our working population and that a minimum of 12 million are children.

That is why the National Health Care Campaign, in which over a hundred national organizations are enlisted and on which I serve as chairman, is urging the enactment of the Kennedy-Waxman Bill which would require all businesses to include provision for minimal health insurance coverage in their package of employee benefits. In most instances, this coverage would deal only with *acute illnesses*. It would represent, however, a genuine step forward in the area of health care, a step which would be due in no small part to a recognition of the fact that health care is an *intergenerational issue*.

One of the most serious gaps in our health care system is the failure on the part of both the public and private sectors to afford any of our generations protection against the devastating costs of long-term illnesses.

The Honorable Arthur S. Fleming is Chairman of the National Health Care Campaign and Former Secretary of Health, Education and Welfare, 1201 16th Street, NW, Washington, DC 20036.

That is why the National Health Care Campaign has been rallying support throughout the nation for the Pepper-Simon Home Care Bill, a bill which would amend Medicare to provide financial support for home care for chronically ill children, disabled persons and older persons. We believe that one of the major reasons for the enthusiastic response this proposal is receiving at the grassroots level is that it grows out of a recognition that the long-term care issue is an intergenerational issue.

Those who have enlisted in the National Health Care Campaign believe, however, that we cannot and should not continue to travel the path of patching our health care system.   .

We believe that the time has come for our nation to join all the other industrialized nations of the world and enact legislation that will provide for universal right of access to adequate health care and that will include provisions for cost containment.

This is the only way to deal fairly and equitably with the members of all generations in the area of health. Older persons are concerned about the inadequacies of Medicare. We are equally concerned, however, about our children, grandchildren, and great-grandchildren who are denied access to any kind of a health care plan (public or private), or who are participating in a totally inadequate plan.

The Commonwealth of Massachusetts has become the first state to enact a law that provides universal right of access to health care to the residents of the State, a law that was passed because it had strong intergenerational support. This action has helped to place the issue on the agenda for 1988 presidential and congressional campaigns. This in turn will help to insure that the issue will be high on the agenda for the 101st Congress beginning in January 1989.

The window of opportunity has opened up for the generations to mobilize and to insist on converting our present unfair patchwork health care system into one that recognizes the fundamental right of access to health care. The determination of leaders of all generations to work together to take advantage of this window of opportunity will break the impasse that has plagued our nation for over fifty years.

Health care is one example, but a major one, of how the generations working together can serve the people of our nation. Each generation is deeply concerned about the welfare of every other generation. We live and work together, often as members of families, and realize, for example, that when government fails to accept its share of responsibility for one generation all other generations suffer. As a result, when judged by its impact, no issue is confined to any one generation. Any movement that seeks to put the generations in conflict with one another is a movement that will undermine the foundation on which our nation rests. My movement which seeks to bring the generations together in order to give the members of all generations the opportunity of achieving their highest possibilities is a movement which will make it possible for our nation to realize its fondest dreams.

A Case for Intergenerational Child Care

Ellen Galinsky, MSEd

It is widely acknowledged that we are facing a crisis in child care. That crisis has its origins in a convergence of demographic factors. In 1940, if a woman with children was employed, she was unusual; only 8.6% of mothers with children eighteen and under were in the labor force. The latest figures from the Bureau of Labor Statistics show that employed mothers are by far the majority. In 1987, 65% of mothers with children nineteen and under worked. Fifty-seven percent of mothers with preschool children were employed, up from 39% in 1975. The most astonishing figures are for the mothers of infants and toddlers: 53% are in the labor force as compared to 35% in 1976.

At the same time, we are in the midst of a baby "boomlet." The baby boomers are having children, thus there is an increase in the numbers of younger children, up from 19.6 million in 1980 to 21.7 million in 1986 (U.S. Department of Commerce, Bureau of the Census, 1987).

The parents seeking child care are having a difficult time. In a nationally representative study that Bank Street College designed for *Fortune* magazine, we found that one out of every three parents of infants and one out of every four parents of preschoolers had difficulty finding child care (Galinsky & Hughes, 1987). In another study we conducted with Resources for Child Care Management (RCCM), we found that 48% of employees with children twelve and under in three New Jersey corporations reported that finding an

Ellen Galinsky is Project Director, Work and Family Life Studies, Bank Street College of Education, Division of Research, Demonstration and Policy, 610 West 112th Street, New York, NY 10025.

adequate selection of child care was a major problem (Lurie, Galinsky, & Hughes, 1987). Most difficult, according to parents, was finding infant care (a big problem for 65%) or sick child care. In a study of five corporations by Fernandez (1986), providing care for sick children was rated at the top of a list of potential child care problems.

Once parents have found child care, it is not just a matter of having one arrangement for each child. In a study by Shinn and her colleagues (1987) at New York University, parents had on the average 1.7 arrangements per child. In the RCCM-Bank Street study, 38% of the families had to contend with over three arrangements for the children in their family.

Studies have also shown that the more arrangements families make, the more likely these arrangements are to break down: the provider resigns or is sick, or the child care program is closed on a day when the parent has to work (Shinn, Ortiz-Torres, Morris, Simko & Wong, 1987; Hughes, 1987). In the *Fortune* study, we found that approximately one-fourth of the fathers and mothers surveyed had to contend with two to five breakdowns in their regular child care arrangements in the past three months (Galinsky & Hughes, 1987).

Compounding these problems, the quality of child care in this country varies widely. In four states, it is legal for one adult to be responsible for seven or more infants. In twenty states, there are no training requirements necessary to provide child care, despite the fact that the carefully controlled National Day Care Study found that when teachers or caregivers had child development related training, the children in their groups fared better socially and educationally (Ruopp, Travers, Glantz, & Coelen, 1979; Children's Defense Fund, 1987).

A final problem is that child care puts a real strain on families' budgets. The less money a parent has, the proportionally higher the child care expenses can be.

These problems have led to a crisis: most parents seeking accessible, affordable, high quality care are behind the eight ball. As a society, we have simply not kept pace with the changes in family life. Unless we reverse this trend, we will be paying for our mistakes. We will pay in higher costs incurred because a generation of children will not have had a developmentally appropriate educational foundation to assume their place as employees in the technologically complex world of the 21st century. As the recent report prepared by the Committee on Economic Development stated:

> Quality education for all children is not an expense; it is an investment. Failure to educate is the true expense. In addition to improving our schools, investing in the careful nurturing of children from before birth through age five will deliver a handsome profit to society and to the individuals and families who have so much to gain.

No one segment of society can take the necessary steps to address this issue alone. It will take the government on a federal, state and local level; businesses both small and large; and the nonprofit and philanthropic community. It will take coalitions. There is one coalition which I see as very noteworthy, bringing together the interests of the elderly and the young. On an advocacy level, groups concerned with issues of the old and young have joined forces to create a coalition called Generations United. This forum has the potential of bringing more clout to the political process.

On a programmatic level, there is an increased interest in bringing together children and senior citizens in two ways. First, child care centers are being established in senior citizen housing and intergenerational centers are opening. Secondly, programs are employing older people as teachers and caregivers; and senior citizens are becoming family day care providers. In fact, a bill introduced into the Senate by Robert Dole calls for the establishment of "Grand Care" programs which would recruit and train senior citizens to serve as child care providers.

At best, it is an ideal marriage; a meaningful connection for both in a society which all too often separates people into narrow age groups. It is an opportunity for older people to do valuable work in a field facing huge labor shortages or to have meaningful relationships that make a difference. It is a positive change for younger people to be with older adults who have the time to care about them and appreciate the everyday moments of their growth.

In our enthusiasm for these efforts, it is important to do the kind of careful program planning that this volume suggests. We cannot assume that just because one has raised a family she or he has an interest in being with children or the skills to care for and teach children in groups. A careful selection process and orientation are necessary. For those older people who become child care providers, training and feedback are also necessary. Payment should be equitable.

Intergenerational programs must have a commitment to make these arrangements work well; it is not good for children to have a large number of adults who come in and out of their lives. One to one connections should be nurtured and supported. If a child has a relationship with an older person who becomes ill, he or she cannot just disappear from the child's life without comment. The situation must be discussed and the child given opportunity to express his or her feelings about it.

Recently, I was on a national television program discussing child care. Afterward, several older people called. One said, "I realized when I heard about child care that this is what I've always wanted to do. How can I begin?" I had a few leads for her, but not enough. Hopefully, expanded intergenerational child care efforts will make a path into this work more accessible. Her dream can become a reality for her and many others, a reality that could reap big dividends for children, their parents, the elderly, and society as a whole.

REFERENCES

Children's Defense Fund. (1987). *Child care: The time is now*. Washington, DC: Author.

Fernandez, J. (1986). *Child care and corporate productivity: Resolving family/ work conflicts*. Lexington, MA: Lexington Books.

Galinsky, E., & Hughes, D. (1987, August). *The Fortune Magazine Child Care Study*. Paper presented at the Annual Convention of the American Psychological Association, New York.

Hughes, D. (1987, August). *Child care and working parents*. Paper presented at the Annual Convention of the American Psychological Association, New York.

Lurie, R., Galinsky, E., & Hughes, D. (1987). Unpublished raw data.

Research and Policy Committee of the Committee for Economic Development.

(1987). *Children in need: Investment strategies for the educationally disadvantaged*. [Executive Summary]. New York: Author.

Ruopp, R., Travers, J., Glantz, S., & Coelen, C. (1979). Children at the center: Summary findings and their implications. In final report of the *National Day Care Study Vol. 1*. Cambridge, MA: Abt Associates.

Shinn, M., Ortiz-Torress, B., Morris, A., Simko, P., & Wong, N. (1987, August). *Child care patterns, stress, and job behaviors among working parents*. Paper presented at the Annual Convention of the American Psychological Association, New York.

U.S. Bureau of the Census (1987). *Estimates of the population of the United States by age, sex, and race: 1980 and 1986* (Current population reports series, p. 25, no. 1000). Washington, DC: U.S. Government Printing Office.

The Intergenerational Movement and Its Relationship to Children and Families: Interview with Margaret McFarland, PhD

Sally Newman, PhD

The following paper highlights the content of a taped interview between Margaret McFarland and Sally Newman (February 1988). The subject of the interview *The Intergenerational Movement and Its Relationship to Children and Their Families.*

MM: "One thing that seems to me to indicate the appropriateness of this whole movement is the breakdown of the extended family unit in our industrial and high tech society to a nuclear family unit which is very different from earlier society. In earlier times, members of the extended family shared appropriate multi-generational responsibilities and functions. This sharing is almost gone now from our society, and I think that the loss of the extended family is one of the very important issues in our time. Let's think for just a minute where we were in the earlier times. You see, the extended family tended to give a lot of support to the development of the identity of each person. Everybody in the extended family knew who the baby was, everybody knew who granddad was, and grand-

---

Sally Newman is Clinical Instructor of Psychiatry at the Western Psychiatric Institute, University of Pennsylvania, Senior Research Associate at the University Center for Social and Urban Research, and Executive Director of Generations Together, 811 William Pitt Union, University of Pittsburgh, Pittsburgh, PA 15260.

Material in this paper is from an interview with Margaret McFarland, PhD, Associate Professor of Psychology, Emeritus, from the School of Medicine, University of Pittsburgh, and Consultant to Family Communications.

245

dad had certain prerogatives, certain responsibilities and certain authority. When you think of Erikson's work and think of his designation of old age as the time of generativity you know that this function is lost from the family today because of the absence of the extended family. It seems to me then that intergenerational programs offer a real replacement for the loss of the extended family and it offers a breadth of experience into the lives of elderly people that comes from being in contact with children at any age.

I think in today's world of the nuclear family, frequently, if the grandparents come and participate in the care of the new generations, there is often a lot of conflict between the birthing generation and the grandparent generation. You see, you can become a grandparent while you are under 40 and still parenting. The deep abiding impulses of care that are part of being a parent, that have multiple gratifications and support the whole sense of worth, may be difficult to surrender as you move into the grandparent generation.

The image of the extended family did not have this same problem because from the earliest times the family had a defined distribution of relationships. I feel that only if the grandparent generation can resign from primary parenthood then grandparenting can become satisfactory. I think this has a great deal to do with the intergenerational programs in the community. If you have a person of grandparent age who goes into a young teacher's class, he/she may feel I could do better or may be very quick to respond to the needs of the children without taking into account the needs of the teacher. It is here that the grandparent self needs to resign primary parenthood and to be free to do the things with the children that they never had time or energy for while parenting. If they don't step back from primary parenting in this situation, there will be constant conflict between the adult generation and also for the child who will be confused by two patterns of mothering or fathering.

I don't think we have explored nearly enough what people being promoted from parenthood to grandparenthood experience, and I feel that out of concern for the grandparent age persons and children in the schools or in other children's institutions we will need to learn about the feelings connected to this promotion.''

SN: ". . . and what about the young mother or young teacher who feels threatened by the presence of an elder? How do we free the birthing generation from feelings of jealousy?"

MM: "It would be a help to the primary parent/teacher if someone clarified that the deep love shared by children and parents enables children to reach out and love another, that being able to extend this love to another is a compliment rather than a threat to a primary parent/teacher. A primary parent should be joyful that their loving parenting taught their child how to extend this love.

I think so much is being accomplished by giving children a grandparent experience that otherwise may not be available to them. I think all of us need to be aware of the life stages of other persons. I want to tell you what children need to learn and I don't see how they can avoid it. Children need to learn how to support and have regard for the infirmities of older people. They need to know that there are limitations in each period of old age, and that persons growing old can do a lot about them. You know I dreaded the possibility that children would be timid about some of my limitations now. But that hasn't been my experience. Children ask you about your limitations but they are not timid or afraid. Older persons need help in learning how to express their handicaps, and they need to learn to be accepting of the inquiries and interests of children.

One of the things that I find delightful and that children and older people have in common is their need to feel needed. Sometimes older people, especially those who may be frail, give children and adolescents a very rich experience by being needed. I would like to see parents dealing more with the longing to be needed by children and older people. Because you know that is what your intergenerational program does, it restores the feeling of being needed. Parents of children in your program need to understand that olders are needed by their children, and that they are not extras. They also need to understand the feeling of their young child "to be needed." Yes, this work restores to older people and introduces to young people a sense of worth and being needed.''

SN: "How do you think we can prepare young children in the next century for a society in which over 20% of a community may be over 55 years of age?"

MM: "Well, I think we must have more projects like Generations Together in which children learn what it means to relate to another person who is not just like yourself, who has skills and energy different from yours. After all, many children have multiple fathers and mothers each with different characteristics and different personalities. We must remember that the outcoming personality of a child will be the result of the child's relationships to mother, father and the supplementary family members who represent positive role models. We must remember that children will be influenced by their relationships to people from all age groups for whom they have had deep feelings.

I had a grandmother when I was growing up who lived in northwestern Iowa and I grew up in Pennsylvania. When I think back on who my grandmother was, she was the one who was there when you had a crisis or if you didn't feel well. She would come and was present when needed. She was the one who would be proud of you when you made a little accomplishment. My grandmother is one aspect of my life that had a very deep influence on my life, on my career choices, on my values, and on my strength. I know without any doubt that my grandmother provided for my sister and for all of us ways of coping with hardship and grief. Grandmother always had a place for kids. My sister recalls that when we as children went to Iowa, Grandmother always had a cookie jar, a real big cookie jar and it was set down where us kids could reach it. When the cookie jar was getting low, she got out her cooking things and made more. And I think I learned a lot about giving and receiving from her through that cookie jar."

SN: "Are the cookie jars still with us in our high-tech society?"

MM: "As long as there are children the need for cookie jars will exist and I believe grandparents, elders and cookie jars will be there."

And so ended the interview with Margaret McFarland, who, throughout her life has been teacher, friend, mentor and confidant to children, parents and students and colleagues in the field of human development.

Index